Walking Out of Spiritual Abuse

Marc Dupont

Sovereign World

Sovereign World Ltd
PO Box 777
Tonbridge
Kent TN11 0ZS
England

ISBN: 1 85240 219 9

This Sovereign World book is distributed in North America by Renew
Books, a ministry of Gospel Light, Ventura, California, USA. For a free
catalog of resources from Renew Books/Gospel Light, please contact your
Christian supplier or call 1-800-4-GOSPEL.

Typeset by CRB Associates, Reepham, Norfolk.
Printed in Canada by Delta Printers, Scarborough, Ontario.

Dedication

I would like to dedicate this book to all those who have, for the love of Jesus, given generously of their time, money, and talents to the Body of Christ only to find themselves hurt, frustrated, and confused. I would also like to dedicate this to Christian leaders who, much to their pain and dismay, have found they have unintentionally hurt rather than healed some of the precious sheep Jesus entrusted to their care.

Acknowledgements

I would like to express much thanks to Julie Thomas for her contribution to the chapter on shame. As always, I am indebted and deeply grateful to my wife Kim for her constant encouragement, grace, and love.

I would also like to thank my parents for choosing to love me unconditionally. Although my mother, Joanne C. Dupont, has not always understood my choice of paths she has always shown love and care. When I was twelve years old she was perhaps the first to ever begin to explain unconditional love to me. She stated: 'To your father and me our children are the most precious things in life.' That single sentence was my foundation in beginning to understand God's unconditional love for His children.

Spiritual abuse, or abuse under spiritual auspices, is the most devastating of all because we are most unprepared and vulnerable to it. With the widespread certainty that in the church we are surely to find all our dreams actualized and our needs met we are suddenly and unexpectedly terrorized by abuses beyond our imaginations.

Marc Dupont, in this book, exposes this dark world with care and tenderness. Those who read from every category will find it helpful and healing. Some will read it who are caught in impossible conditions who do not even suspect abuse and are blaming themselves. For them hope will rise. Others, without knowledge, are actually engaging in behavior, which is or will be producing such abuse as herein described. For them, hopefully, this book will prove a warning trumpet and a reason for reversal. For others the ominous episode of abuse is past but the results are residual. For these, perhaps more than any others, this book will prove a healing balm. For all of us reading this book will hopefully be an experience of walking through pain to the Father's heart and excitedly moving from being a part of the problem to becoming a part of the solution in this dark and devastating world.

Jack Taylor
Dimensions Ministries
PO Box 189
Melbourne FL

I have known Marc Dupont for seven years and he has been a part of our leadership team at TACF since May, 1992. His life experience and years of itinerant work, interacting with hundreds of churches and leaders, have qualified him to approach this sensitive subject. Marc is very experienced in bringing wisdom and encouragement to both victims and leaders who have been caught up in toxic faith. Bringing God's people into His freedom is a key message of the hour. I heartily recommend this book to you, both for yourself and for friends who are needing to come free from spiritual control.

John Arnott
Senior Pastor
Toronto Airport Christian Fellowship
Toronto, Ontario

Contents

Foreword

Marc Dupont's book, unlike other books on spiritual abuse that I have read, goes directly to the problem of abusive churches. His first chapter, 'Why Do Abusive Churches Exist?' analyses the story of 'Henry'. Such churches exist because of the potential for sin in us all, sin that results from the Fall of humankind. Both abusive pastors, and the churches that abuse their pastors, have a common cause.

The story of Henry begins the book. It is the story of how Henry became an abusive pastor. Marc finds the roots of Henry's subsequent deterioration in his home life. Raised by an alcoholic and largely absent father, the story of Henry's salvation is a wonderful and heart-warming one, but his rise to pastoral power has hidden pitfalls because of his upbringing – or lack of it. His insecurity and his need for the congregation's approval cause him both to coerce and to manipulate them. What led to his father's alcoholism leads to Henry's coercion and manipulation. In another book I call this idolatry/witchcraft.

Marc then proceeds to analyse the story of a church in which spiritual abuse also occurs. At the same time he looks at the life of Jesus which, unlike today's diplomats and politicians, publicly displays great firmness and an indifference to public opinion. For instance, he cursed the Pharisees with a sevenfold curse (Matthew 23:13–36). Christ's security arose from His own relationship with the Father, so that if we are to inherit the degree of security we see in Messiah's life, we must first know in all its fullness the Father's redeeming love for us. Otherwise the transparency of Jesus will be impossible for us.

At the end of the book Marc adds a couple of chapters about God's forgiveness for pastors who are into spiritual abuse. God forgives us as we humble ourselves before Him. In one chapter Marc describes the jezebelic pride of a woman who assumed that hearing from God entitled her to instant obedience to 'God's' orders. Yet she herself lacked the virtue of humility.

We all have the tremendous potential for sin in us which can manifest itself in many ways. There are warning signs for pastors so that they will know what to look out for in themselves lest they become like Henry. In some areas of the world, deacon and elder 'boards' find it easy to keep pastors under their thumbs. Abuse can exist either way – to pastors – or from pastors to others. It is described in Scripture and God plainly hates it – probably more than any other sin.

John White
August 1997

Introduction

God is a god of authority. He desires His children to respond to His inherent authority out of love. He also delegates His authority to leaders in many areas of life, including church. Leaders however, are human, and so there is always the potential for the misuse of authority and power.

This is not an anti-authority book. If anything it is pro-authority, but **biblical** authority. More than that though, it is concerned with ministering out of the wholeness of God the Father's heart. Jesus stated that:

> 'the good man brings good things out of the good stored up in his heart, and the evil man brings evil things out of the evil stored up in his heart. For out of the overflow of his heart his mouth speaks.' (Luke 6:45)

A primary focus of this book is to understand that if God's love is not the heart motive for church leadership, then abuse of power and authority is likely, if not probable.

Abuse is the **misuse of power.** Whether the abuse is emotional, physical, sexual, or spiritual it is always about the wrongful use of power and authority. Power used by an individual to control, manipulate, and/or use another. The end result for the victim is damage. It may be physical harm, emotional harm, sexual harm, spiritual harm, or a combination of those. Abuse is always about those with power or authority using their power or authority wrongfully in order to compensate for their fears, hurts, and insecurities.

Although abuse is always wrong, in some cases it is more gravely wrong – especially in those cases where a sacred trust is betrayed, such as between a parent and a child or a spiritual leader and a disciple. It is not only wrong because of the misuse of authority and immediate harm to the victim, but it is deeply wrong because basically it is betrayal. It is betrayal of the child, or the follower, who by the very nature of the relationship is usually very trusting and somewhat dependent on the one with power. In such cases the long-term effects of betrayal can, in fact, be ruinous to the overall mental and spiritual health of the victim for the rest of their life if healing is not found. Subsequent relationships with friends, loved ones and potential friends and loved ones can often fail to ever reach the true potential of love and trust. This betrayal and hurt can rob the victim of the freedom of trusting and choosing to be vulnerable again.

The ultimate tragedy of abuse by either a parent or a spiritual leader is that if not cared for and healed, the victim will find it difficult, if not impossible to completely trust God. Because both parents and pastors are to a degree representations of God's fathering and Jesus' shepherding in our lives, a warped view of love with authority, will carry over into our hearts a wrong understanding of God – despite what our theology may be.

I first became aware of abuse by being involved in counseling in the early 1980s. At first I thought it was a simple matter of faith. Sure, some had been hurt but if they would simply choose to believe the Bible and trust in God's inherent goodness, He could begin to redeem the hurt. But as I began to pray through some of the issues with victims of abuse I found that they did have faith – or they would not have come in for counseling in the first place. Perhaps a passage of scripture that more than anything else convicted and convinced me that there was a need for more than encouragement, was Jeremiah 6:13–14. It reads:

'From the least even to the greatest
Everyone is greedy for gain;
From the prophet even to the priest
Everyone practices deceit.
And they heal the brokenness of the daughter of My people
      superficially,
Saying, "Peace, peace,"
But there is no peace.'

The fact that God repeats this two chapters later in Jeremiah 8:10–11 emphasizes His great concern for those who come to Him vicariously through His shepherds and are used rather than truly cared for.

Much of the preaching and teaching I did throughout the early and mid 1980s was centered around the freedom of the cross for each of us to be led by the Holy Spirit and practise intimacy with God. But in ministering in many churches around the world I found that often because of either religiosity, egocentricity, or personal hurt in the lives of church leaders, the people of the church were being short-changed. In fact, often not only were they not permitted to really flow in the biblical freedom of the Holy Spirit, but they were being used as pawns or tools to facilitate the leader's goals. Often those goals, even though dressed up in biblical words and vision, were simply the leader's need to 'be somebody' and 'be successful'. In other words, these leaders were often abusing and using people in their churches to compensate for the hurts and bondages in their own hearts. Sometimes, the abuse would simply be theological ignorance of the value God places on each individual. In the Kingdom of God each individual has intrinsic value, as opposed to communism which, birthed out of atheism, sees the individual's worth only as a means to an end.

'A little knowledge is a dangerous thing.' To my great surprise, disappointment, and frustration I began to realize that several friends of mine and church leaders whom I respected, were inadvertently abusing people. To make matters worse, I began to see some characteristics and potentials of abuse in my own ministry. By the late 1980s at least two churches that I regularly ministered with, on opposite sides of the globe, had blown up due to heavy pastoral abuse. Both of these churches had great potential of reaching many lost with the gospel. They were both very dynamic churches in their community. What was shocking was that in both cases I knew these leaders. I knew that they were not pastors who would ever deliberately do what they had done. But because of my itinerant involvement with these churches I knew that a lot of good people, including friends of mine, had been severely messed up.

The first spiritual abuse seminar I did was amazing! The crowd was not huge, perhaps about 400 people or so. But despite being involved for many years in many strong conferences and seminars I don't think I had ever seen quite the hurt revealed in peoples lives before, except in cases of sexual abuse of children. And what really grabbed my attention was that the symptoms of those spiritually abused were similar to those who have been sexually abused. The room was filled with people who loved God. Many of them came from a wide assortment of churches and had given their lives, so to speak, to serving their churches. Yet many of them were filled with deep pain, anger, resentment, shame, and confusion. I realized at that time that the need of healing for spiritually abused Christians was not a minor, but a major area of ministry, and one in which the Lord truly desired to work.

My hope is that those who have been used and/or abused by church leaders would find in these pages a deeper understanding of God's healing grace – both for themselves and for those who may have sinned against them. For leaders who realize they have, inadvertently or otherwise, used people to facilitate their vision, my hope is that their first call to ministry – to heal the broken hearts and set the captives free – could be fully restored, or perhaps become their foundation for ministry for the first time. As Paul wrote to Timothy:

'It is a trustworthy statement: if any man aspires to the office of overseer, it is a fine work he desires to do.'
(1 Timothy 3:1, NASB)

But unless that desire stems from the heart of Jesus who did not come to be served, but rather to serve, the fruit will be mixed.

Marc A. Dupont
Toronto, Ontario
May, 1997

Chapter 1

Why do Abusive Churches Exist?

Perhaps the most perplexing question concerning the whole issue of spiritual abuse in the body of Christ is: how can a truly spiritually alive church possibly be abusive? How can it be that people who know the truth and acknowledge Jesus Christ as Lord and Savior could fall into this dilemma? Are there actually born again people who would deliberately desire to hurt and control others in the family of God? Fortunately, the answer is usually no. Most leaders who end up with a harsh and demanding style of leadership are not individuals who would **deliberately** hurt others. The problem is more complex than simply good leaders versus bad leaders. The problem is rooted in the very fall of humanity in the beginning of history.

In the Garden, mankind was represented by Adam and Eve. We are all descendants, not only physically but spiritually. The apostle Paul stated that *'the first man Adam became a living being'*[1] but also *'in Adam all die'*.[2] Adam and Eve's sin was to be a reflection of all of humanity. Whether we are as we are because we are their descendants or whether their sin was a symbolic response for all of us is an intriguing theological question. But the point is we **are** fallen in nature. The key to spiritual abuse lies in understanding what the original sin really was.

Adam and Eve were naked and unashamed before God and one another. Most of the time when people in the Bible are either putting on or taking off clothes it is symbolic of the freedom to be transparent, or real, with God and others. Adam and Eve would meet with God in the cool of the day, between two and four in the afternoon, after the high heat was past. The situation was one of intimacy and grace. A relationship with God not based on works but love and freedom. The freedom to intimately know and to be known.

When Satan as the subtle snake came to them, his goal was to rob man of intimacy with God. The first lie was to plant seeds of doubt in Adam and Eve's minds concerning the spoken word of God: 'Did God really say to you?' The second lie was that Adam and Eve could be **as** God if they would eat from the forbidden fruit. If Adam and Eve could obtain enough knowledge they could be as God, and be in control of their lives. Instead of a child-like trust in their relationship with God, they could through knowledge direct their own destinies. Rather than resting in God's love they could be gods themselves.

Adam and Eve as representatives of humanity bought the lie. They did gain knowledge of right from wrong, but the knowledge was perverted because it was outside the domain of God's grace and lordship. The true sin was, and is, that humanity prefers to be in control. Unfortunately this is also true of many Christians. There are many who totally believe in Jesus' salvation, but find it very hard to believe in a father/child type of relationship even though Jesus said we must be both *'converted'* and *'become as children.'* We find it very hard to do what Proverbs 3:5 instructs: *'Do not lean to your own understanding but trust in the Lord with all your heart.'* Jesus stated in John 16:13 that He would send us the Holy Spirit who would *'guide you into all truth. He will tell you what is yet to come.'*

Despite the exhortations in the Bible to trust and rest in God's goodness, provision, and protection we, as Christians, often determine our lives the same way that non-Christians do: by the dictates of man's wisdom as opposed to the leading of His Spirit. A Christian can believe in Jesus, live by biblical morals, and look forward to heaven but still not seek the face of God and His specific direction.

Israel Deserved King Saul

This leads to the opportunity for spiritual abuse, and is best pictured in 1 Samuel chapter 8. The elders of Israel came to their main prophetic leader – Samuel. They told him that like the nations around them, they would like to have a king. Samuel was upset by their request because he realized that the Lord God Jehovah was in truth their King, but the people insisted saying, *'that we also may be like all the nations, that our king may judge us and go out before us and fight our battles.'*[3] As Samuel prayed, the Lord instructed him to give them a king. They had not rejected Samuel, but rather had rejected the Lord from being King over them.[4] This is a corporate picture of what took place in the Garden with Adam and Eve.

Two things stand out here. One, the people preferred to have a leader they could look at and put into perspective from a human viewpoint, even though they believed in God and wanted His blessings. Two, even though the Hebrews were God's people, God gave them the choice of rejecting His Kingship over their lives. He would not abandon them or withdraw His love, but He allowed them to choose the less-than-perfect option of looking to, and trusting in man for leadership rather than Him. Samuel went on to warn the people that if they did have a man as a king, he would be very costly. He would take their best sons and daughters to serve him in his army. He would take a portion of their livestock and their produce. Samuel told them that the situation would become so costly that they would rue the day they had not trusted in God's invisible but true Kingship over their lives.

The man they ended up with as king was Saul. From outward appearances Saul looked the part of a true king. Saul was a choice and handsome man. 1 Samuel 9:2 states that there was not a more handsome person in all of Israel. He was also the tallest of any of the men of Israel. To outward appearances he was a great king. Inwardly, however, Saul had some serious defects. He was not really a man fit to be a leader. He suffered from cowardice as well as greed. We all fight fear to a degree, but Saul's fear of man and failure was overwhelming, as 1 Samuel 13 shows. His unbelief in God's goodness and protection would often prevent him from leading Israel against their enemies in obedience to God's will. His insecurities also caused him to stumble in following God's directions. Instead of destroying all of the booty in the victory against the Amalekites he saved the best of it for himself.

Proverbs 30:22–23 states: *'The earth can not bear it when a slave becomes a king.'* When a person with bondages such as rejection, fear, envy, greed, or lust, comes into power and prestige, that person can often be easily manipulated by their hurts and chains. Unless there is a strong foundation of personal trust in God's goodness and protection, there is usually an attempt to cover up the weaknesses. We tend, like Adam and Eve did, to compensate for inward fear and insecurity with control and manipulation. Jesus, in contrast to Saul, said in John 14:30 that Satan had absolutely no hold within Him with which to manipulate Him.

The Story of Henry

Henry grew up with an alcoholic father. His father was a good man in many ways but because of the hurts and insecurities of his own childhood, he never was able to give demonstrative love to Henry. Henry never heard his father tell him that he loved him or that he was proud that Henry was his son. Also, because of the alcohol, Henry did not experience consistent provision from his father. Henry's mother was a good woman, but because of the hurts from the marriage and having to work full time in order to make ends meet, she was too busy and too tired to give Henry the supervision he needed as he was growing up.

By the time Henry was 14 he was doing drugs. By the time he was 15 he was stealing to try to stay in drugs. By the time he was 17 he was using girls physically. The idea that sex was for a sacred relationship made no sense to him because his parents' marriage had been such a complete disaster. Because of the vacuum of love in his family his appetites for acceptance and comfort were strong and perverted. He lived for the moment, as the future held nothing worth working towards. But when Henry was 19 and beginning to really despair about life, everything changed. He met Christ!

Henry's conversion made a great testimony because it was one of radical change. One day he was stealing, doing crack, and sleeping with girls, the next he was reading the Bible and telling all of his friends about Christ. When Henry had reluctantly attended that first church service he was quite unexpectedly overwhelmed by the Holy Spirit. For the first time in his life he was experiencing unconditional love in a powerful way. He knew he had found the reason for life and living – Christ.

Henry quickly became a pastor's dream disciple. He was eager to learn, he was giving and serving sacrificially, and his passion for Jesus was obvious to all. Henry became one of those natural evangelists who are attractive to almost everyone, because his love for God and others was genuine and not a facade.

After three years of faithfully growing in the Bible, serving in the church, and doing street evangelism Henry went off to Bible School. Henry's pastor and others saw leadership all over Henry because of the depth of his commitment to God and His Word. Henry did well at Bible School. He studied hard. His teachers and fellow students were all encouraged by Henry's commitment to be a radical Christian. This was the only way Henry could live because he knew beyond a shadow of a doubt that he had not only been on his way to hell, but had actually experienced hell. When

Jesus got hold of him he was completely aware that he owed everything to God's grace and mercy. He loved God with abandonment.

Henry, not unusually, met a girl at Bible School who was also deeply in love with Jesus. Unlike Henry however, she had grown up in a healthy Christian family. Both of them wanted to serve God all of their lives. They both felt led to start a church and do a lot of evangelism after Bible School.

The first several years after Bible School were great years for Henry and his wife. They had a baby girl and a baby church. The money was tight so Henry worked 30 hours a week selling cars, but he didn't mind because it gave him the opportunity to meet people and talk about Christ. The church began to grow. People were attracted to Henry's simple but focused Bible studies about God, God's salvation, and blessings. People in the church were drawn to work alongside Henry in the outreaches to the community because of his contagious enthusiasm for the lost.

By the time Henry was in his early 30s many thought he was on top of the world. His hard work had paid off and the church had grown steadily to about 300 people. Many of them had been won to Christ through Henry's effective preaching of the gospel. The church had its own attractive building and offices. Henry and his wife were at the peak of health and had three wonderful children. Henry was respected by other Christian leaders in the community. Even those pastors that thought Henry too simple in his preaching or too radical in his zealousness appreciated and respected him. There was just one problem: Henry was a wreck inside.

The problems for Henry had first begun when the church began to grow past a small home group. There were now major questions and problems that he was faced with. Questions about how to prioritize the church money and how to work with the growing number of gifted Christians that were beginning to attend the church. Henry began to find that despite his theology concerning God's love as the ultimate reward he was very scared that others would look better than he in their ministries and functions. In his mind he felt that if the church did not prosper in numbers and money, the other pastors in the community would not respect him as much as he desired. He hated it when other pastors whom he had just met would ask him the dreaded question: 'How big is your church?' Although he was glad about the growth, he longed to be one of the big boys in town with a church of 500 to a 1000 or more.

As time went on, Henry began to be suspicious of those in the church who seemed more gifted in certain areas than he was. His assistant pastor, Jim, was a gifted communicator and teacher. Henry allowed him to preach less and less out of jealousy. He assumed that when others complimented Jim they were really saying they preferred Jim's ministry to his own.

To his dismay, from time to time others on the leadership team would become overly tired and ask for a break for a season or so. Henry was great at motivating people, but had never understood that Jesus is both Lord of the Harvest **and** Lord of the Sabbath. So when Henry began to hear talk about burnout, he began to preach sermons rebuking laziness and lack of vision. Henry began using terms like 'rebellious', and talked of lack of commitment to those that were the most committed in the church. In short, Henry was beginning to be more and more of a slave to old fears. As his personal bondages rose to the surface he increasingly spoke not out of treasure stored in his heart, but out of fear and control. Satan had, indeed, waited for an opportune time to manipulate his old weaknesses.

Henry had always been ashamed when he saw other kids at school wearing new or nice clothing. Because of his father's alcoholism the family seldom had a good income. They mainly survived because his mother worked as a secretary and cleaned houses on Saturdays. So when Henry's church began to have a steady amount of money coming in, Henry insisted on a salary that was well beyond the 100 or so people the church had in attendance. By the time the church was 250–300, Henry insisted on a big showy house and matching car. His idols were some of the preachers on TV who were always seeing a great harvest of souls, together with a great harvest of money befitting someone so anointed by God. As a boy and young man he had needed to work for or steal everything he enjoyed. He could not understand that God could want to love him simply because he was His adopted child. Because his relationship with his human father had been deficient in expressed love and time spent in friendship, he interpreted God's love as material blessings for this realm and heaven for the hereafter. He felt that spending time relaxing or having fun with Christians was pointless, aside from strategizing and praying for more numbers.

Finally, tired of the accusations and growing tension and distance between themselves and Henry, Jim and his wife left the church. They were extremely ambivalent about it because they loved Henry and his vision. But, they were realizing that Henry only saw people from a utilitarian viewpoint. People who they loved were being increasingly hurt by the constant pressure of living up to Henry's demands.

Jim and his wife leaving was the straw that broke the camel's back. Over the next 12 months over half the church left. The more key leaders and tithers that left, the more bitter and self-righteous Henry's sermons became. The further Henry receded from his goal of being a great, successful leader, the more fearful and insecure he became. The more his fears and insecurities increased, the more he compensated by being forceful and manipulative. Henry had preached many times on Jesus' lesson from the last supper regarding learning to be a servant of all. But as he was gripped more and more by fear of failure and feelings of inadequacy he became more and more of a tyrant. As members left the church to attend other churches in the community Henry became more distrustful of other leaders. Often he began to berate and attack other churches and movements from the pulpit.

The people that stayed on were no longer a group of

outgoing visionaries who were glad to serve and give. They were cowed by Henry's manipulative sermons and directives. Mainly they were the ones who needed discipleship and healing themselves. An objective counselor would have said they were individuals who, because of poor self-images, were vulnerable to living vicarious lives through a hero. They were basically in the same condition as a man with a bad paying, dead-end, hopeless job and lifestyle, who lives for rooting for his football team on Sunday afternoons.

Because of Henry's preaching they felt that it would be a shallow love for them to ask for help or ministry themselves when there were so many needy people out there. They were confused as to why so many leaders had left, but they were also sure Henry was truly God's man because of the wonderful anointing on his life. The idea of seeking God and asking Him what church they should be at or what ministry they should work at never entered their minds. Why should they question Henry? He looked, sounded, and ministered like a real Christian hero. He was a 'head taller and more handsome' than any of the other leaders in town. After all when he preached and prayed for people things happened. People got saved and healed, and wasn't that what church was all about?

Henry's church never really bounced back to its high point. The numbers tended to fluctuate between 75 and 150. Every time they would go through a growth spurt Henry would talk about the 'fresh move of the Spirit coming over the Church' and rally the people to pray more and work harder. When the numbers began to slide back down Henry would rave from the pulpit about spiritual warfare and people being deceived by the enemy. Often Henry would publicly denounce those who left saying they were rebellious and breaking covenant. After three years of the up and down cycle happening repeatedly, the church went down to 30 people and could no longer afford to pay Henry a salary or the church mortgage. With great anger and frustration Henry quit the ministry and went back to selling cars. He was quite successful and made good money but he seldom witnessed, and often resorted to alcohol to take him through the low points much as he had before he came to Christ. The ones who had stuck it out to the end found it hard to integrate into other churches. They found that in general they now had a rather blasé view of church and the kingdom of God. They still loved God in their hearts but found going to church brought intense feelings of guilt, fear, and emptiness. Most of them continued to live their lives by biblical ethics but found themselves apathetic at best when thinking of church and the body of Christ.

The tragedy for Henry was that he truly loved God and people. But because he was a slave to hurts, rejection, and fear of failure the enemy had hooks in him. Luke wrote that when Satan stopped tempting Jesus, he waited for an 'opportune time' to come back and try it again. Henry, unlike Jesus, did have vulnerabilities. It was much more advantageous for Satan to wait until Henry was powerfully influencing 300 people or more, than to come after him in full force when he was a young man full of zeal but with little influence. In studying the kingship of Saul, we see God sending him David – an unlikely 'giant killer' from the sheep fields. Rather than receiving David as a gift Saul began to be increasingly jealous of David, even though he appreciated his gifting, especially in music. Both Henry and Saul are pictures of men who were kings outwardly but slaves inwardly.

The tragedy for the people of that church was that God never intended for them to be ruled by 'a slave'. Most of the victims were innocent in that they did not understand that at the center of God's will is His heart for His children. His love for us is not a utilitarian love based on our performance. Rather, it is intrinsic and unconditional. He does not value us for what we can do for Him, He values us because we are His children created in His image and purchased by the blood of Jesus.

With Henry as with King Saul, the tragedy is doubled. First because the people were hurt, but secondly, because they did not need to be hurt. The sin was as much the people's as it was Saul's or Henry's. If Israel had listened to Samuel, they would have looked to God as king rather than man. If Henry's church had sought God about submitting to his ministry, God would have warned them. He would have directed them to a church and leader who was not merely a visionary, but who would as a true shepherd not blow out the flickering wicks and break the bent reeds.[5] As Jeremiah 29:11 states:

> ' *"For I know the plans I have for you," declares the* LORD, *"plans to prosper you and not to harm you, plans to give you hope and a future."* '

All too often we are swayed by outward appearances. Saul **looked** the part of a king. Henry **did** lead people to Christ and heal sick people. The problem was, that because of his hurts and insecurities, his true vision for the Kingdom of God was choked out by his need for the kingdom of Henry.

Henry is a fictional person, but parts of his story unfortunately are common occurrences in real life 'toxic faith' churches. Any obvious portrayals here in part or in full of any past or present churches and/or leaders are purely coincidental.

Notes

1. 1 Corinthians 15:45: *'So it is written: "The first man Adam became a living being"; the last Adam, a life-giving spirit.'*
2. 1 Corinthians 15:22: *'For as in Adam all die, so in Christ all will be made alive.'*
3. 1 Samuel 8:20.
4. 1 Samuel 8:7.
5. Isaiah 42:3.

Chapter 2

Testimonies

An inherent part of the problem with spiritual abuse, is that we are hesitant about having negative thoughts towards church leaders that we believe in. Usually, those who are very involved in abusive churches are somewhat trapped because of isolation. They are afraid to think out loud, or ask questions regarding any concerns they may have, for fear of being viewed as critical or divisive. This isolation, much like the sexual abuse of children, robs one of the ability to put the picture into true focus. Instead, a hazy religious lens tainted by guilt, manipulation and shame, dulls our understanding. This chapter may be unnecessary for some. For others these accounts will help put some of your own views, experiences, and hurts into a clearer perspective.

The following two accounts took place in a medium-sized church in the mid-west of the United States. Due to the fact that the overall situation has never really been brought to a conclusion, the true names of individuals, as well as the church have not been used. It also needs to be stated that the following accounts are the personal views of two individuals who were severely hurt by the process. That is to say that these accounts are biased. What is important to realize however, is that often in these types of situations, what hurts is not only what happened, but our perceptions of what happened. When abuse in any form is not fully brought out into the light, Satan can and will use the hurt

and rejection to rob us of true communication. Without com-
munication with those who offend us and with those we offend,
we are robbed of the whole truth and the ability to see the
situation from each other's positions.

The first account is 'Suzy's' description and views of what
happened to her. Suzy had a multi-church counseling ministry in
her city. She joined the church just after the first signs of burn-out
and abuse began to be visible. Although she was not a titled
leader, such as a pastor, or elder, she was given both responsibility
and visibility by the leadership.

The second account is from 'Ted'. Ted was one of the assistant
pastors with the same church as Suzy. He gives us a brief
description of his perspective of the church both at the time and
in retrospect.

Suzy

> *'Nevertheless, I have this against you: You tolerate that*
> *woman Jezebel.'*   (Revelation 2:20)

It was late Saturday night when the phone rang. I was out of
town, studying in my hotel room in Virginia, preparing to
take a certification test with the Association of Psychological
Type. On the other end of the phone was my longtime
friend Jim calling from home. I was startled to hear his voice
at such a late hour. I was ten hours from home and I knew I
didn't give my phone number to anyone other than family.
Something devastating must have happened in order for
him to find me and make a call. As he started to talk, my
heart began pounding so intensely my chest ached. It took
all I had to hold onto the phone as he began telling me
about the bizarre and coercive meeting he had just attended.

Jim was frantically summoned by our pastor late Saturday
night to attend an **emergency** leadership meeting at the
church. When he arrived, Jim described the atmosphere in
the room as 'frenzied, like a pack of wolves waiting for the
kill.' The pastor distributed a six-page document full of

'accusations with evidence' regarding my character and reputation titled *Charges Against Suzy Townsend*. He read Matthew 18 and lectured them on church discipline. He then told them I had 'refused to meet' with the leadership so they 'must take action immediately' to save the church from this 'evil spirit.' The meetings in question had been presented to me with very short notice. They were to take place during a time when I was doing my final preparation for the above-mentioned examination. In addition to my studies, I was also working that week and needed to drive eight hours to the place of testing. A corporate decision **had** to be made **that evening** because I was 'either a wolf or completely deceived, unrepentant and a danger to the church and the leadership.' The pastor orchestrated a plan to use the church discipline process to denounce my actions and present my 'sins' publicly to the congregation the next morning.

My life, as I knew it, was about to change forever. While listening to Jim, my teeth began to chatter and my body began shaking as I reeled with questions: What was happening? What did I do? Why were they doing this? Why didn't anyone talk to me? Who could allow such bizarre behavior? A whirling tornado of trauma and fear enveloped my being. How could a church that was once vibrant and alive, decay into a controlling and manipulative system ... spinning out in violent chaos? All I could think was 'this must be what it feels liked when one instinctively knows they are about to die.' My life would never be the same again.

Jim, his wife Joan and I have been friends since college. The three of us, and many other dear friends, were all very involved with this new church plant. Our church was 'on fire' and part of a new movement that was experiencing anointed worship, music and giftings. Our pastor had a tremendous vision for his church and the community. This was a fulfillment of a 'life vision' he had since his youth. We were all very invested in what the Lord was doing in our city. We traveled together to Scotland and England on a ministry trip and attended several conferences on the west coast. It was exciting, even exuberant at times, to be connected like we were. The church was rapidly growing and maturing. What we didn't know was so were the problems.

What happened the next morning was like a scene from a nightmare. Three hundred people filled the church expecting to worship and have fellowship. Only those who attended the meeting the night before knew the hidden agenda for the day.

While I was out of town and without my knowledge, I was going to be put on trial for committing 'spiritual crimes' against the church. In my absence, I was summoned to perform the role of my life. The script was prepared and brilliantly written. The pastor, unknowingly to others, had spent the last few months secretly and selectively compiling a list of 'accusations with evidence' regarding my character and ministry. The role I was to portray in this performance was the **scapegoat**. I was the chosen one, the person who was being blamed and slaughtered for the chaos and loss of control within the dysfunctional family (church) system.

No one, not the assistant pastors, or the kinship leaders, or any of the members of the congregation really understood what was about to happen to our church. We were very trusting and naive, like a young child with his parent. No one knew that we were about to participate in and witness the most insidious form of spiritual abuse; a pastor who, I believe, would violate his ecclesiastical power to control and manipulate and shame his congregation in order to secure his position and lust for power.

That morning the service began with the pastor informing visitors that this would be a day of dealing with 'family issues' and that if they wanted to leave they could do so. A six-page dissertation of the 'seven sins' I had supposedly committed was distributed to the congregation. An entire two-hour Sunday morning service was dedicated to my 'church discipline' and the 'wrestling against the principalities and powers, against spiritual darkness in high places, against demonic forces that come to divide the church and basically bring death to all of our lives.' (And that would be me.)

In the sermon, I was described as rebellious, unteachable and unrepentant. I was called 'either a completely deceived Christian or wolf in sheep's clothing' and accused of the most insidious things. The overriding crime I had committed and the intentions of my actions were to 'demasculate the leadership and destroy the church.' I was called a **Jezebel**, 'the spirit they had been fighting since the inception of the church.'

Each of the three pastors, and a guest speaker from Florida (another pastor from the same movement), took their turns depicting my horrific crimes. They accused me of:

1) 'Promoting non-biblical teaching.'
2) 'Encouraging digging into the past for the purpose of getting well.' They believed that the 'individual should not focus on getting healthy and well by looking at their past, but rather focus on the Lord Jesus Christ only and pursue Him.'
3) 'An unbridled tongue.' One major characteristic of a Jezebel spirit is the use of flattery. I was accused of 'lying and using flattery to manipulate the pastor.'
4) 'Lack of submission to and trust of leadership.' They described this by saying they 'have yet to see a submissive, brokenness and teachableness that accompanies a repented heart. This is what we want, and this is what we are looking for.' What I believe they were looking for was shame, a total submission to their authority and leadership because they were 'God's anointed and appointed leadership.'
5) 'Encouraging separation.' I was accused of recommending books to read without them being submitted to church leadership. Also, they believed I encouraged separation because I somehow 'manipulated the worship leader to step down and take time off from his anointed position.' They interpreted his choice to spend more time with his family as an influence by a Jezebel

whose characteristic is to 'control and destroy the anointing on the worship leader.'

6) 'An Arrogant Attitude'. They believed that in 'some of the statements she made, Suzy needs to come to repentance on. Some of her statements do nothing to promote the unity of the brethren. It tears it down. It creates dissention and disunity.'

7) 'Walking in agreement with darkness and deception.' They somehow knew I had collaborated with a 'demonic force that has tried from the inception of this church to wrest control and direction over the leadership.' I had willfully 'allowed access to demonic spirits to bring division and sow discord among the fellowship.'

My words and motives were manipulated, distorted and displayed publicly as facts. Two hours were spent defaming my good name and character. I was publicly slandered, humiliated, shamed and exposed in front of my friends and colleagues, my church and community. I was accused of promoting divorce, division, darkness, deception and labeled a 'Jezebel'. What happened that day was sick and twisted and untrue. The only truly remarkable fact from that morning was I wasn't even invited to, or informed about, my own funeral.

The service ended with the pastors repenting of their 'sins'. They were sorry they released my ministry into the body and did not provide proper oversight. Communion was reserved until the end so everyone could properly cleanse themselves of all sin. The pastor's wife lead worship with *Purify My Heart*. So began 'Suzy-gate'.

'Woe to you, teachers of the law and Pharisees, you hypocrites! You shut the kingdom of heaven in men's faces.'
(Matthew 23:13)

That day, my life would change forever. Trauma, fear and isolation replaced trust, respect and relationships. The trauma I have experienced due to the abuse of spiritual power and control has been catastrophic. The pain and shame I have suffered has been massive and immobilizing, the losses almost unbearable.

It has taken me over five years to diagnose and label what happened to me emotionally, physically and spiritually. I watched my life, and the lives of many other good Christian people, fall apart and break into a million pieces. We are still trying today to understand and pick up the pieces.

Spiritual abuse is a horrific crime. It murders the soul and causes trauma in the deepest crevices of the heart. It violently shatters the human spirit, breaking trust at the very core of one's being. Accompanying the trauma and hemorrhaging pain, innocence is lost and a sacred trust is betrayed; a trust that may never mend in a world that no longer seems safe.

I am telling my story for several reasons. One, I was unaware that spiritual abuse even existed until that day. It is a subject that churched people do not want to talk about or admit that it happens. Spiritual abuse in a church is kept a family secret. No one wants to talk about 'the pink elephant in the room' and expose the lies because the consequences can be very severe for telling the truth.

It took several years to understand and label the deep devastation and trauma I was experiencing. My symptoms were identical to the symptoms of those who suffered from sexual or physical abuse. How could this possibly be? Was I abused? Ken Blue, a pastor in Southern California, explains very simply that abuse of any type occurs when someone has power over another and uses that power to hurt. Physical abuse means that someone exercises physical power over another, causing physical wounds. Sexual abuse means that someone exercises sexual power over another resulting in sexual wounds. And spiritual abuse happens when a leader with spiritual authority uses that authority to coerce, control or exploit a follower, thus causing spiritual wounds.[1] I had no comprehension of the deep and devastating wounding that can occur due to the trauma of spiritual abuse. Now I know. If it happened to me, it can happen to anyone.

Secondly, my prayer is that my story will create an awareness of the symptoms and damaging effects of spiritual abuse. My hope is that my story will validate and encourage those who have had similar experiences.

> 'Men never do evil so completely and cheerfully as when they do it from religious conviction.'   (Pascal)

I returned home a week later after finishing my course work in Virginia and teaching a seminar in Cincinnati. At the time, I was working in a hospital at an in-patient adolescent treatment center. I'd just recently left a Christian Counseling Center where I counseled, presented seminars and developed marketing and public relations plans. And I was busy building a consulting practice through teaching communication courses in local churches. The knowledge of my public lynching had already traveled far and wide. My life, personally and professionally quickly came to a screeching halt. There wasn't a single person in my life that was unaffected by the brutal attack on my character.

My pastor contacted the pastors in local churches where I was teaching and informed them of my 'sins' and the church discipline service. Several members of an informal pastoral council of non-denominational churches within the city were contacted. These pastors and leaders met together on regular basis to pray and support one another. They were all told about the 'Jezebel spirit' and the errors of my ways. No one in the Christian community ever contacted me to teach again.

My mentor at the Counseling Center, Dr Riggs, called and asked what had happened to me. She had an appointment with a client on Monday morning. Her client had attended my church for the first time that infamous Sunday morning. The client was recovering from a previous experience with an abusive church and was hysterical. The client described in great detail what was said and done to a woman named **Suzy**. I was mortified. The director of the Counseling Center sent me a list of the warning signs to look for in a cult. My colleagues obviously had discussed the situation and thought I was involved in a cult! I was professionally ashamed and humiliated.

My best friend's husband was a pastor at the largest church in the city. Most of my Christian friends from college attended this church. I felt so embarrassed when he asked me to explain what had happened. I was an intelligent professional woman from a healthy family. How could I have let myself get involved in something so bizarre and destructive? I didn't have an answer. I just looked away in shame.

I received a letter from Beirut, Lebanon from some very dear missionary friends of mine. That week, they received a phone call warning them about my situation. When they wrote, they asked if I had slept with the pastor! They couldn't imagine what else I could have done to cause such widespread trouble. Pastors in various states across the USA were contacted and told why the church had to 'publicly discipline' me. Even friends I've known for a decade questioned my character after attending this service. They eventually cut me out of their lives.

The trail of shame and humiliation was never-ending. I will never ever forget the day I went to get my hair cut. When I walked in the front door, the hairdresser looked up at me and acted as if she had seen a ghost. She was petrified and afraid and wanted nothing to do with a 'Jezebel'. I walked away, mortified and ashamed. There wasn't a place I could go where I didn't feel exposed and rejected.

No one from the church leadership ever contacted me when I returned home (except for one 'form letter' that in the ensuing break-up of the church the senior pastor sent out to many people. It was somewhat apologetic, but only in broad terms. There was not one personal attempt from him to reach out to me, that I know of). I was shunned, cut off and left hanging out to dry. Almost everyone, except for a few very brave souls, were too afraid to call or contact me. I was treated as if I had a deadly and contagious disease. The message was very loud and clear in the sermon that Sunday, 'even if Suzy gets everything patched up, it is my hope and prayer that this (evil spirit) doesn't spring up in **you** or a **number of you!**' These are very powerful and frightening words to hear from the pulpit. What if it was true? What if he does to me what he did to her? It scared everyone into silence. Sadly, the valuable relationships I built through the years were absolutely destroyed.

Four months after the July church service, I moved home to Cincinnati. I literally could not function living in that city any longer. The shunning and humiliation affected every aspect of my life. I could no longer consult or teach anywhere. I felt professional shame and embarrassment. I felt my friendships were either so broken and completely destroyed or damaged so badly they were too difficult to repair. I was numb and in shock and traumatized at the very core of my being. It was so difficult to understand what was happening to me emotionally, physically, and especially spiritually. I didn't understand that I was having the same reactions as someone who had been raped.

I tried to walk away and minimize what happened. However, I couldn't deny the facts. What was happening to me, and to my body, was extremely severe. Medically, I was diagnosed with post-traumatic stress disorder and depression. For several years, getting up and going to work each morning was virtually impossible. I was wiped out every day by three o'clock. The only way I was able to semi-function for several years was by taking anti-depressants. Thank God I found a wonderful Christian therapist who was knowledgeable, who understood, and could explain to me what was happening. It felt as if I had been in a life-threatening accident and I was left all alone on purpose to die.

I was also diagnosed with chronic fatigue syndrome. My system just wore out with all the stress and trauma. I gained seventy pounds in two years. One only had to look at me to see how I stuffed all my pain. Although I was comatose and numb to most of my feelings, my body could not lie. It's not an exaggeration that I've spent thousands of dollars on counseling and medical bills in the last five years. I could go on and on.

> *'If I cry out concerning wrong, I am not heard,*
> *If I cry aloud, there is no justice.'* (Job 19:7)

The most confusing aspect of this entire nightmare, was that I just didn't understand it. I didn't have the language to describe spiritual abuse. I never knew it even existed. No one validated the insanity of it all. Where was the truth? Why wasn't anyone talking? That makes you feel even more crazy. Did this or didn't this happen? Was it this bad or wasn't it? Was there a 'pink elephant in the room' or wasn't there? The entire twisted charade was mismanaged and ignored all the way up the system. The validation of what happened to me, and to many other dedicated and caring Christians, was virtually ignored by the leaders in the system. Mostly, there was only the hollow sound of silence.

Elie Wiesel was a holocaust survivor and is an international advocate for its survivors. In Germany, he delivered a famous speech to the President of the United States, Ronald Reagan. He said,

> 'I have learned the danger of indifference, the crime of indifference. For the opposite of love, I have learned is not hate, but indifference. Jews were killed by the enemy but betrayed by their so-called allies, who found political reasons to justify their indifference or passivity. What have I learned? When there is obvious injustice and principles are violated – when human lives and dignity are at stake – when your allies find reasons to justify their silence or indifference – neutrality is a sin.'

There was tremendous power and healing for me in this statement. The passivity and indifference in the church was almost more painful that the act itself. It is dangerous to be indifferent when obvious injustice and principles are violated. When human lives and human dignity is at stake, when leaders find reasons to justify their silence or indifference, it is a sin. Martin Luther has a similar quote:

'No matter how faithful we claim the word of God, if we remain silent in the very area someone is attacking us, we are not proclaiming the work at all.'

Both of these men obviously experienced great pain. Silence only sanctions others to become abused.

'Toxic faith is a destructive and dangerous relationship with a religion that allows the religion not the relationship with God, to control a person's life.'
(Stephen Arterburn & Jack Felton)

So what went wrong? How did a once vibrant and growing church decay and end its life by controlling, manipulating and abusing its members? What actually happened to cause this pastor to make these destructive decisions and destroy the spiritual lives of so many? Was it really something evil, like a Jezebel spirit, that took over my mind and caused all the destruction? I don't think so. In fact I now know the truth.

A church family is vulnerable to the very same emotional problems and stresses that our families are susceptible to. Life can become very difficult at times. Church life can be difficult too. Change, growth, fear, insecurities, even success can pile more demands on the 'family' than it knows what to do with. The leadership in a church can feel afraid and out of control and desperately tries whatever works, functional or dysfunctional, to manage the system. If a person never learned how to cope with his/her overwhelming feelings, religion can become the addiction, like any other drug, to manage and medicate the pain. It's the emotional health and decisions we make during these difficult times that can bring 'death or life' to the entire family.

In their book, *Faith That Hurts, Faith That Heals*, Steve Arterburn and Jack Felton explain how a church family can take on the same symptoms, characteristics and roles of a dysfunctional family. A person can misuse their faith to avoid reality and responsibility. Their intent is not to worship God, but to alter their perception of reality. They are driven by a perfectionism that causes them to attempt to earn favor with God through striving harder. Religion, not God controls their lives.[2] A deceptive and twisted, manipulative and shame-based form of religion slowly seeped into our church. That's not how we started out. And that was certainly not the intent of the senior pastor. But, over a period of time we became blind and deaf to the fact that we could no longer hear the love and grace of God. The mission became size and numbers, and began to totally replace a genuine concern for people and relationships.

The way we began to communicate within our church family diluted the truth even more. Open, honest conversation became almost dangerous. Family secrets of sexual abuse and manipulation had to remain a secret. We communicated through an unwritten code of religious 'family rules'. These unwritten rules were intended to conceal family imperfections, keep the family looking perfect and protect the parents (pastors and leaders) from facing their own personal problems. The rules are:

1) be blind, to your own perceptions of reality and to the mixed messages you see and hear;
2) be quiet, to the abuse that's going on in order to protect the parent (pastor);
3) be numb, to your feelings and your personal boundaries;
4) be careful, to trust anyone too much because you will always get hurt; and
5) be good, to obey and look perfect at all cost. Never ever question the authority of the parent (pastor).[3]

Dr Martin defines an abusive church as:

> 'A group or movement exhibiting a great deal of excessive devotion or dedication to some person, idea or thing. Employing unethical, manipulative or coercive

techniques of persuasion and control designed to advance the goals of the group leaders to the possible or actual detriment of members, their families or community.'

In a nutshell, this is what happened in our church.

Our theology and doctrinal viewpoints were correct; we believed that Jesus Christ was the risen son of God. It wasn't our creed that was unsound, it was the deed because the psychological and emotional health of the leadership was imperfect. As Jesus stated:

> 'The good man out of the good treasure of his heart brings forth what is good; and the evil man out of the evil treasure brings forth what is evil; for his mouth speaks from that which fills his heart.' (Luke 6:45)

To acknowledge that the Christian church is spiritually abusive is very difficult for many people to admit. No matter what you want to believe, the reality still exists. The abuse of spiritual power and control in the church is a horrific crime. Abuse is the misuse of power, whether sexual, physical or spiritual. Spiritual abuse will not be stopped until the myths about it are recognized as myths, and until the people in positions of power and influence understand the real meaning of and motives behind spiritual abuse.

Jesus understood. He called the spiritually abusive scribes and Pharisees; hypocrites, blind guides, serpents and a brood of vipers. Outwardly they appeared beautiful and righteous, but inside they were full of uncleanness, hypocrisy and lawlessness. The spiritual leaders of the day shut off the kingdom of heaven from men and women and neglected the weightier provisions of the law: justice and mercy and faithfulness (Matthew 23). The mission in our church, if we chose to accept it, was to fulfill the vision of the pastor. To build his kingdom come, on earth as he thought he had heard from heaven. He was the one who was receiving the glory, honor and praise forever, Amen.

I don't think it was an accident that a few verses before Jesus exposed the Pharisees, He answered the question:

> '"*Teacher, which is the greatest commandment in the Law?*"
> *And He said to him,* "'**You shall love the Lord your God
> with all your heart, and with all your soul, and with
> all your mind.**' *This is the great and foremost command-
> ment. The second is like it,* '**You shall love your neighbor
> as yourself.**' *On these two commandments depend the
> whole Law and the Prophets.*"' (Matthew 22:36–40)

A Pastor's Experience and Perspective

*'Ted' was one of the assistant pastors at 'Suzy's' church. The
following is not only his view in retrospect of what happened to
Suzy, but how the church gradually dominated not only his
discernment but some of his basic biblical values as well.*

We came from an evangelical background having served 11
years on staff with a para-church organization. Our association with many different denominations and practices of
belief were many. So when we made the transition to a
church that was part of a newer movement it wasn't done
blindly. Our introduction to it came from some close friends
who were also on staff with the same para-church organization. They were later forced out of the organization because
of their involvement with 'signs and wonders'.

At that time we felt there was something lacking in our
Christian experience. As we studied our Bible there seemed
to be something contradictory in what we saw in scripture
and what we were experiencing day to day. As we discussed
this with our friends during a trip up to their part of the
country they shared with us the exciting things God was
showing and teaching them. We were eager to hear about
their experiences and soon found ourselves looking into the
whole arena of signs and wonders and body ministry.

We discovered shortly after that there was a new church

forming in our city and we decided to visit to see what it was like. As we drove up to the house where they were having a small group meeting, I remember telling my wife, 'If it gets weird, we're out of here!' It was just the opposite. We had a very nice time meeting some people who had a lot in common with us and who shared similar evangelical backgrounds. We decided to try it out a few more times. Within a few weeks we found ourselves really enjoying being a part of this small group of people and wanting to help plant the kind of church they were talking about – one where we don't just talk about the works Jesus did but one where we all actually go out and try to do the same things as well.

Our family and the pastor's family had become very close friends during this time even before we went on staff with the church. We spent a great deal of time together as families and enjoyed each other's company. We really believed God had called this man to come and plant a church in the city and that this church was going to have a significant impact on the city for Jesus. Coupled with the specific vision God had given him was his charismatic teaching. We were ready to follow Jesus through this man and help be a part of God's plan for this city. This was the first step in forming an unhealthy relational situation. We slowly moved towards allowing his charisma and anointing to dominate our own spiritual discernment and biblical knowledge to a very unhealthy degree. To be fair, this was as much our fault as anyone else's.

As the church grew, we became more heavily involved in the leadership of the church and eventually joined the staff as an assistant pastor, overseeing the Worship ministry, church administration, and pastoral oversight. The church continued to grow and be an exciting place to be. We quickly grew to a 'membership' of about 400–450 people.

On the surface everything looked great. People were happy and excited about what was going on. Sunday services were growing, and God seemed to be moving in people's lives in powerful ways. Underneath, the rumblings of something wrong were beginning to appear. People in leadership began to withdraw from responsibility, some prominent people were leaving the church, and tension was mounting on the senior pastor and his wife. People who were having problems, were labeled, or perceived, as not being fit to travel the same road where God was leading.

During my time on staff I began to see problems. I started to disagree with the direction of where things were headed or how things were being handled. Unfortunately, I didn't confront the pastor on these matters because he was the one with the vision for the church. To disagree with him was like disagreeing with God. I was so eager to follow God I wouldn't dare disagree with God's appointed leader, so I kept silent. It almost cost me my marriage. I became more committed to the church than I did to my wife and I sided with other leaders even when I didn't agree with what they were doing. I would come home and complain to my wife about future plans or activities and then say nothing. I couldn't bring myself to confront issues. After all, who was I? I wasn't the one God called to plant the church.

During this time a young lady named Suzy came to our church who had a growing counseling ministry. As leaders, we welcomed her into our congregation. She quickly integrated with several people in leadership including the pastor and his wife. Suzy began sharing out of her counseling experience with some key leaders in the church. At the time it looked as if the senior pastor was going to have her head up a counseling ministry within our church. I remember having several meetings discussing this option.

A number of other things were happening during this same time period. A new group of people had come into the church who were getting involved on the leadership level. We hired another assistant pastor. At this time there was a nationwide movement in the 'Prophetic'. People were saying that 'God told them' that the senior pastor had some special position in the area to see the gospel go forward and our church grow at an incredible rate – like he had much much higher calling than a normal pastor. Other pastors from other churches were looking to him for direction for the city. At the same time the pastor was showing signs of breakdown. He commented to myself and the other associate pastor on several, maybe seven or eight occasions, how he just wanted to teach and train and not involve himself in the everyday affairs of the church. He began to hide himself in his office, leaving decisions to us assistant pastors more frequently. He reversed decisions almost daily, in particular about how the church was to be governed, and by whom. Concerning Suzy, one day she was going to head up the counseling ministry in the church, the next day she was a Jezebel trying to destroy the church with her teachings.

There were other signs of control and manipulation taking place though that were disturbing. The senior pastoral couple began to be overly concerned about what women in the church wore – which culminated in a women's meeting in which the women were forbidden to wear crop tops, short skirts, etc. Also at least two women were informed that their body types were causing the pastor to 'stumble' and would they please refrain from certain postures (i.e. raising their arms up) when he was around! There was a general reactionary mode going on always, like everything that was done had a fear motivation.

There was a polarization happening among people involved on the leadership level. It was as if people new to the church core were vying for the power positions while those who had helped plant the church were becoming aware of the toxic system they were involved in and began withdrawing from their roles. This emerging pattern was seen as evidence of Suzy's growing detrimental influence over the body.

In general Suzy and her teaching/counseling were often mentioned as the root problem. At one point, three of the main couples in the church had a meeting with the senior pastor, his wife, my wife, Suzy, and myself. They brought forth a list of complaints against us about the church and how we were running it. These complaints were disbelieved and Suzy was further vilified as the ring leader. The denial/scapegoating syndrome was growing more and more prominent. The couples left the church after several attempts at communicating with the pastor on the issues.

Some of these well-trusted couples were soon dismissed by the senior pastor as not ever being fully on board or fully trustworthy. Rather than listening and discussing whether their questions were valid or not, they were simply perceived as somewhat rebellious. In the meantime, other couples were coming forward with accusations against Suzy as advocating 'unbiblical teachings' (i.e. recommending divorce to a woman in an abusive marriage, encouraging digging into the past for the purpose of getting well, encouraging lack of submission to and trust of leadership, 'unbridled tongue'). The senior pastor was at such a low stage emotionally, he had the other two pastors meet with the people who had the complaints. He was still vacillating on where he saw Suzy – our church counselor or a Jezebel.

Finally, the senior pastor decided we needed to meet with Suzy to discuss these issues. There were attempts to meet but they were unsuccessful. The senior pastor communicated to us that he had talked with Suzy and communicated the seriousness of the situation. I was asked to get in touch with her to set up another meeting. Suzy, on short notice, said she would meet with us on a Saturday morning. When it was time to meet a message was left saying she would not be able to meet with us because of a prior commitment she could not break. That evening the leaders and small group leaders of the church, met in order to discuss this serious situation. We discussed all the details of what had transpired up to that point and discussed what course of action should be taken. It was decided to call Suzy to repentance ... at the Sunday service the next morning! Personally, I wasn't sure what the right thing to do was at that time. It seemed a harsh thing to do but I was so caught up in the religious system that I wasn't able to think for myself. And I was still trusting that God would give us wisdom as to what was the right thing to do. I was wrong in allowing the pack mentality to prevail rather than trust what I really believed. There was only one couple who was willing to stand up and say we were doing the wrong thing and that we should give this matter more time. Unfortunately, as a church we lived in crisis mode most of the time – this could not wait. The enemy was at the door waiting to destroy the church through something (or someone like this).

The next day was an awful day for me and I believe many others. Almost the entire service was given to the matter of Suzy and the charges brought against her. She was asked to come to repentance and come in and meet with us about the matters at hand. Fortunately for her, she was not even in town that day. I think instinctively we knew this wasn't the right thing to do but we went ahead with it anyway. I have deeply regretted that day ever since.

As a result of this issue, the growing emotional breakdown of the senior pastor, several unsuccessful attempts by the senior pastor to release the church to others who were in a better condition to oversee it, and the relational breakdown among the pastoral team, we decided to resign from the church. It was one of the most difficult decisions I have had to make in my life. I was in ministry for 15 years and thought that was what I was supposed to do with my life. But after seeing the damage done to people's lives in this church I could no longer support the pastor or his leadership. I also began to question my motives for being in ministry. As a result of these issues my wife and I lost several close friends in the church. There was also a split within the church – those siding with the senior pastor and those who didn't. People couldn't understand how everything could turn so badly so quickly. To make matters worse there was no arena or opportunity to discuss all that had taken place so there was a great deal of misunderstanding within the church as to what the real problems were. People blamed Suzy for all the problems, others blamed the assistant pastors for trying to take the church away from the senior pastor, others blamed the senior pastor. The system was a mess.

After we resigned from the church we made whatever attempts we could to reconcile the relationships that had broken down. The first one we concentrated on was with

Suzy, and then on the other close friendships that were damaged. It was very painful work because it forced us to deal with issues in our lives that we either chose to disregard or were blind to. Either way, it was painful to see how we had been abusive to others while all the time thinking we were helping them get closer to God. It caused us to take a closer look at what we had come to believe doctrinally, and came to the conclusion that at least parts of that religious system have distinctives of a cult; particularly in the devotion required toward the main leader, and because of some of what we now believe are not biblical teachings. Fortunately, I can say that over time most of the damaged relationships have been reconciled and we are once again friends with several of the people. I pray I will not ever let religion, no matter how exciting or seductive, steal my common sense and simple devotion to Christ . and my family, again.

Notes

1. Ken Blue, *Healing Spiritual Abuse*, Intervarsity Press, 1993, pp. 12.
2. Arterburn, Stephen and Felton, Jack. *Toxic Faith: Understanding and Overcoming Religious Addiction*, Thomas Nelson Publishers: Nashville, 1991, pp. 31–36.
3. Arterburn, Stephen and Felton, Jack, *Toxic Faith: Understanding and Overcoming Religious Addiction*, Thomas Nelson Publishers: Nashville, 1991, pp. 31–36.

Chapter 3

Jesus – A Servant with Authority

'The goal of our instruction is love from a pure heart.'
(1 Timothy 1:5)

One could assume that Jesus' style of leadership was laid back and casual. A leader who would never give strong directives, or rebukes. This view is perhaps popular in today's culture due to the increased distrust of authority in the last few generations. An anti-authority mind-set can cloud our perceptions of Jesus' inherent and delegated authority. In addition, if an individual does happen to fall into the trap of spiritual abuse, their views of authority are often so undermined that any pastor who does more than simply **encourage** the flock must also seem to be abusive and out of God's order.

The reality of Jesus' leadership style is quite different however. In fact, when one reads the Bible, it is impossible to get away from the demands of God for obedience. This is not just an outdated Old Testament principle. Jesus in the beginning of His ministry said, *'Do not think that I have come to abolish the Law or the Prophets; I have not come to abolish them but to fulfil them.'*[1] In John 14:15 He stated, *'If you love me, you will obey what I command you.'* Jesus, in Matthew 16:23 saying to Peter, *'Satan get behind Me,'* is certainly not the picture of a leader afraid to direct or rebuke. The beginning of Matthew 21 contains the story of Jesus instructing the disciples to borrow a donkey without asking permission which in one sense is tantamount to stealing. Jesus was far from being a leader afraid or unwilling to exercise authority.

Does this mean that leaders who are heavy-handed and who attempt to dominate the lives of their followers, are merely leading in true Jesus style? No, it does not. In order to understand Jesus' relationship to His disciples it is first necessary to understand His relationship to the Father. In fact, it is necessary to come to a biblical understanding of what love is and isn't, correctly understand, measuring our love for Him by our obedience to Him, and the implications of that in church life.

The Motivation of Jesus

The basis for everything Jesus did was love. Firstly, love for God the Father and secondly, love for humanity. In the story of the women at the well in John 4 the disciples returned to Jesus. They had made a short trip into the village for food, and were very surprised to see Jesus speaking to this Samaritan women for three reasons. First, a good Hebrew would not be seen speaking to a Samaritan. They were viewed as wayward cousins so to speak, in the religious community of the times. A normal Hebrew would cross over to the other side of the street in order to avoid a Samaritan. Secondly, this was a Samaritan women. A good Hebrew man especially would not want to be seen with a Samaritan women. It was deemed beneath them. Thirdly, this woman especially one would not want to talk to. She had been married five times and the man she was living with now she was not married to. Her lifestyle was probably reflected in her face and her clothing.

The disciples attempted to draw Jesus away from the woman by saying that the meal was ready to eat. His classic response to their (not His) dilemma was, *'I have food you know not of.'* He had something at hand that He found even more nourishing and fulfilling than a good meal after journeying all day. He qualified that food as, *'to do the will of the Him who sent me and to finish His work.'*[2] This is an extremely important passage in understanding Jesus' heart and motivation. It defines His *modus operandi*, His impetus for everything He did on earth.

If He had only indicated that His food was to minister, or to serve others, it would not tell us the whole story. His motivation was not just to serve others, but to be a servant to the Father; the one who sent Him. John 3:16 reads:

'God so loved the world that He sent His only begotten son (Jesus).'

In Philippians 2:6–8 we read about Jesus:

'Who, being in very nature God, did not consider equality with God something to be grasped, but made himself nothing, taking the very nature of a servant, being made in human likeness. And being found in appearance as a man, he humbled himself and became obedient to death – even death on a cross!'

He was a servant to humanity, but first a servant to God the Father. The apostles John, Peter, and Paul, in their writings, often refer to the Father as *'the God of our Lord Jesus Christ.'*

Jesus served the Father out of love. That statement can be easy to understand, but the depths of His love and service are hard to grasp in our times of quick divorces, misplaced loyalties, and lack of commitment. The most poignant picture of the depths of His obedience was in the Garden of Gethsemenae. In the first garden, Eden, mankind so quickly rejected obedience in favour of self-centeredness. In the second garden, Gethsemanae, Jesus preferred the Father's will to His own even though it was clear through His labored prayers, that the directives of the Father were far from being His own choices. Out of love He lived as a servant.

Love is the grid through which authority must be understood, just as God does not deal with man only with His holiness, but with compassion also. If that were not so, all of humanity would be completely doomed. The same is true of His authority. All authority in heaven and on earth has been given to Jesus by the Father, but His hand of authority is always directed by His heart of compassion and grace. Hence, we find in 1 John 4:8, God defining Himself as love. Just as His mercy triumphs over judgement, so His authority is released in the context of love.

If we biblically examine the motivation for not only what Jesus did, but for all service we constantly find the impetus of love. According to Luke, the writer of the book of Acts, Jesus stated, *'it is better to give than to receive.'* This comes out of the very nature of the Father. For the purpose of love He takes the best that He has, in our case Jesus, and out of love sends Him to die on a cross for us.

In 2 Corinthians 9:7 Paul is talking about the proper motivation for giving money. Money is always a key insight into the heart of man. Money is a human standard or index by which many people measure the difference between survival or prosperity. Most people plan their lives by their financial status. Money equals security to most. Jesus told more parables concerning money than any other topic, precisely because it is so important to us, and how we handle it, is a true reflection of our hearts.

Paul states:

> *'Each man should give what he has decided in his heart to give, not reluctantly or under compulsion, for God loves a cheerful giver.'*

Reluctantly means unwillingly or against one's real desires. Not under compulsion means not under manipulation. To be manipulated means to comply with someone out of fear, flattery, or guilt. It is very biblical to fear God, and that fear should in many situations cause us to obey Him. But God's will for us as we move into a more mature relationship is to obey out of love rather than out of fear for the consequences of doing our own thing. Perhaps the most clear-cut definition of grace is that God's grace renders us the power and freedom to do what He desires us to do, rather than to do what we want to do and get away with it.

One of the common traits of an abusive Christian leader is the use of manipulation to get something from the church or audience. Visionary messages are preached about everyone becoming involved and contributing, while liberally condemning those who would hesitate. Pleas for financial contributions are often underscored with the manipulation that if one doesn't give the ministry will collapse. It is interesting how often those who make such statements are often great teachers about faith in God's provision. This is not to say that church leaders should not make the needs known to the congregations. But that can be done matter of factly, trusting God to speak to the people, rather than by using fear or guilt.

Love is a Choice!

The answer to the age-old question of why God allows sin and suffering, always has to do with love. God desired humans created in His image to freely love Him and desire to know Him intimately. As humans created in God's image, we have a built-in generic need and desire for others to love and value us from their hearts. Perhaps the most clear instance of Jesus desiring love out of choice rather than fear from His disciples, is in John chapter six. Due to Jesus' message that people would have to *'eat of His body, and drink of His blood'* a lot of His popularity had ceased. In fact many of His disciples had stopped following Him. Jesus addresses the questions and doubts the twelve may have of Him in John 6:67.

Most of us in that situation would have made strong

49

statements to stir up faith and commitment. Many would have made manipulative statements such as, 'You owe Me, I've given My best to you twelve.' Or perhaps we would have tried to get our desired results through fear by saying, 'The Father gave you twelve especially to Me, if you don't stay with Me now you will be breaking covenant and bringing judgement down on yourselves.' An appeal to the greater vision might seem in order; 'There's too much at stake here for you guys to leave over this minor misunderstanding.' But Jesus, rather than making any sort of manipulative statement at all, simply **asks** them, 'You do not want to go away also, do you?' He very clearly gives them the choice of whether to stay or go. He wants them to stay, but He wants them to stay because they want to stay even though they were chosen first of all by the Father.

God in His heart desires sons and daughters who obey out of love, rather than slaves who obey out of fear. Paul sums this up in chapter 8 of the book of Romans. The book of Romans is possibly the most important theological book of the New Testament, with chapter 8 perhaps being the heart of the book. Verses 14 and 15 read:

> '...those who are led by the Spirit of God are sons of God. For you did not receive a spirit that makes you a slave again to fear, but you received the Spirit of sonship. And by him we cry, "Abba, Father."'

The true measure of a son of God is not outward legalistic sacrifices but rather a child-like obedience from the heart.

Because God is love, according to 1 John 4:8 and 16, God desires obedience as a response of love. This is the lifestyle Jesus lived. Even as a child growing up He stated to Joseph, *'don't you realize I must be about My Father's business.'* In Matthew 18:3 Jesus states that we must not only become converted but that we must become as a child if we are to enter into the kingdom of heaven. To be 'converted' or 'born again' to attain the free fire insurance is not God's perspective of the gospel. It is to enter into a child-like relationship with the Father. Jesus constantly modeled this. We read in John 5:19–20 and 8:28–29 Jesus saying that He only did what He saw the Father doing. In fact, He said that He did nothing of His own initiative. He loved to please the Father; that was His life and goal.

Jesus' Security and Significance

In Luke chapter 3 verse 22 we see two things of great importance taking place in Jesus' life. First the anointing of the Holy Spirit came on Him in the form of a dove. Secondly, the Father spoke and said that He not only loved Jesus, but was well pleased with Him. Both of these were of critical importance for Jesus to experience before His ministry began. He needed the anointing of the Holy Spirit if He was to minister in power being both fully human as well as fully God. Secondly, in facing the loneliness, rejection, and persecution to come He needed the ongoing communication of the Father's love and approval.

Every human being has two basic emotional/spiritual needs; a need for security and a sense of significance. That is, we need the sense that our lives are going to work out okay and in addition we need a sense that we are of value at least to close friends and family. When good relationships and security are lacking we resort to all sorts of means and fixes to compensate. Jesus however, needed no outward fixes. He was so loved by the Father that He walked in great freedom. Freedom to be and do all that the Father called Him to despite the threat to Himself. He was not afraid to lose followers or popularity. He was not afraid to suffer violence or even death. In His case, 1 John 4:18 was perfectly fulfilled:

'God's perfect love drives out fear.'

The issue of our foundational motivation for ministry will be discussed in a later chapter, but at this point it is necessary to understand why Jesus was the type of leader He was. He was willing to take incredible risks, not only with His own life but also with the church. He was willing to give the twelve disciples the choice of continuing on or leaving Him. The strength for this type of freedom lies in the fact that even as He loved the Father the Father loved Him. In Luke 3:22 the Father states, *'You are my Son, whom I love; with you I am well pleased.'* When Jesus appears in glory on the mountain of transfiguration with Moses and Elijah, again, the Father states, *'This is my beloved Son, with whom I am well pleased.'* According to the rather prophetic Psalm 2, the Father instructs the Son to ask of Him for the nations and He will give them to Him, as well as the ends of the earth as an inheritance. Even in this Father–Son exchange we see the Father requesting the Son to ask Him for this inheritance.

In John 13 Jesus stated that knew He had come from God and was returning to God. He states, in John 14:30, that the prince of the world, Satan, was coming but had absolutely nothing on Him (Jesus). Jesus' life, His peace, and His security were all determined by His relationship with the Father. Because that love was complete there were no strongholds of fear or envy that caused Jesus to become the slave of anyone or anything. He was not dominated by fear of rejection, or the impulses of the populace, because He knew where He came from, who He was, and where He was going. He was not a slave to His ego and He had no need to see His disciples obeying His every whim out of fear of His temper. He was, in fact, the first perfect, or whole, human being alive. Adam and Eve had tasted of that type of love but out of self-centeredness they had lost it.

Cleansing and Being Cleansed

The last supper was Jesus' final opportunity to teach the disciples before the arrest and crucifixion. Jesus said to them, *'I have longed to have had this supper with you.'* He began this final lesson by washing their feet as a lowly servant would have. If we remember Jesus' response to the disciples dilemma while he was speaking to the Samaritan woman, He said He had food they knew not of. Again, while at a meal, He is teaching them about a more nourishing food than they knew – dying to self.

> *'You call me "Teacher" and "Lord", and rightly so, for that is what I am. Now that I, your Lord and Teacher, have washed your feet, you also should wash one another's feet.'*
> (John 13:13–14)

His point wasn't that leaders should not lead with authority, but rather that leaders in leading should have the motivation of a servant.

On a final note in examining Jesus' motivation, it is significant to look at the timing of when the Father voiced public approval of Jesus. The first time, in Luke 3, took place after Jesus had submitted to the baptism of John. John's baptism was one of repentance for forgiveness of sins. When John saw Jesus coming to him and recognized who He was by the Holy Spirit, he protested by stating that he was the one who needed baptism by Jesus, not Jesus by him. When John protested, Jesus stated, *'Let it be so now; it is proper for us to do this to fulfil all righteousness.'* Why would He say it was necessary for all righteousness when He (Jesus) had no personal sin? Simply because He recognized that John was still the 'man of the hour'. He was still the Father's chief spokesperson for the Kingdom of God. Even though Jesus Himself had created John as well as all of humanity He not only recognized the Father's authority on John but submitted to it. He had no guilt whatsoever which would have rendered repentance necessary. But His heart was focused on much more than the law. His heart's desire was always to honor and please the Father. Even when that meant submitting to a created being. It was after that submission to the Father's delegated authority in John that the Father spoke His pleasure in His Son and anointed Him to soon begin His public ministry.

The second occasion was at the mount of Transfiguration. This occasion, as recorded in Matthew 17, verses 1–8, took place shortly after Jesus had begun to show His disciples that He was going to go to Jerusalem and suffer many things and then be killed (Matthew 16:21). Rather than following something as significant as His baptism, this time the Father's approval came in preparation for His coming ordeal. The Father is, at least in a small private meeting, voicing His love and approval of Jesus. Again, 1 John 4:18 states, *'perfect love casts out fear.'* Love is not a static relationship with the truth, even though one can love truth and principles. Rather, love must flow through the give and take context of a relationship. Jesus had by now spent two years or more in public ministry being led by the Spirit to do the Father's will. Now Jesus is beginning to face the most difficult and challenging time of His life on earth. The Father, rather than simply directing Him, is filling Him up afresh with the ongoing communication of His delight in His Son. Jesus' impetus, or motivation, is being strengthened for the trials ahead.

The overwhelming law of relationships in God's kingdom is love – meaning obedience by choice. That is why Paul stated God has not given us a spirit of slavery taking us into fear again, but rather the spirit of adoption. All true leadership in the Kingdom, must have the impetus of Jesus' love for the Father. Not grasping for significance or security through reputation, power, or money derived through ministry. A true leader leads with authority, but that authority if it is true authority comes from the Father for the purpose and increase of love. Love for the Father and love for the people that the Father loves.

Notes

1. Matthew 5:17.
2. John 4:34.

Chapter 4

The Father Heart of God – A Foundation of Love

In the previous chapter we examined Jesus' motivation for doing the things He did. In this chapter, we will examine in detail God the Father's heart for relationship with each of us as individuals. It is only by living in close relationship to the Father that Jesus' lifestyle can truly be emulated.

If a room full of Christians were asked to write down a one sentence definition of eternal life there would be many different answers; living in mansions on streets of gold would be one. Another might be never being sick again, or no more tears of sorrow or disappointment. Others might say no more work. Many would certainly say not having to go to hell. Most would say 'being able to see Jesus face to face.' All of these answers would be true. What is important however, is how Jesus would define eternal life. In John, chapter 17 which contains Jesus' prayer to the Father, He states in verse 3:

> *'This is eternal life, that Father they might know you and the Christ whom you have sent.'*

God has always been a God of relationships. Even though He is complete in and unto Himself, His essence – love – is to share Himself with others. In Hebrew numerology, the number 3 is the number symbolic of perfection. God is three persons in one. Deuteronomy 6:4 reads:

> *'Hear, O Israel: The Lord our God is one Lord.'*

He is one God, but three persons, or a triune God: God the Father, God the Son, and God the Holy Spirit. In Himself He has not only perfection of being and creation, but perfect, or complete fellowship. But always with God, His deeds must be understood through the scope of His heart. God is love according to 1 John 4:8. Love cannot be measured by depth of thought as opposed to action, despite the valuing of knowledge over experience present in many evangelical churches today. The Bible is very clear that love is measured by action, rather than knowledge.[1] Our values must be established from our theology, but our values must lead to living, not merely thinking. The post-modern world today is filled with philosophers, psychologists, psychiatrists and teachers educating us about life but who often cannot keep their own marriages together, and are relationally dysfunctional. The Bible, God's word, continually makes the point that true love is measured by action and reaction in the context of relationship.

In several Old Testament passages God refers to His relationship with Israel and Judah as a husband and wife relationship. In Genesis 2:24 God spoke of the marriage relationship and said:

> *'Therefore shall a man leave his father and his mother, and shall cleave unto his wife: and they shall be one flesh.'*

It is to be a relationship of deep intimacy. Not merely the physical aspect, but a sharing of the inner man and woman. The apostle Paul, in his first letter to the church in Corinth warned against sexual fornication on the grounds that by so doing a Christian is defiling his or her body because it is a temple of the Holy Spirit. He stated that if we are in fact people born again by the Spirit of the Living God, it is God's own Spirit which is within us. The picture of the man and women cleaving together in marriage is a picture of us as individuals cleaving to and being one with God by His Spirit, according to Ephesians 5:31–32. We are individuals, but at the same time we are indwelt and to be filled with God's Spirit. While we are still in a less than perfect condition the union with the perfect, complete Triune God has begun. All this is to say that God is a God who desires great intimacy with His people – the Father with His children and Jesus with His bride. In fact, according to James, God *'jealously desires the Spirit which He has made to dwell in us.'* God is jealous over anything that has a greater hold of our hearts than Himself.

As with a healthy marriage, where there is not only a physical intimacy but an in-depth heart to heart transparency, so that is God's intention for intimacy with His children. Paul states in the book of Romans chapter 8, verses 14–15 that:

> *'...all those who are led by the Spirit are the Sons of God...'*

and that we

> *'...have not received a spirit of slavery taking us back into fear again, but we have received a spirit of adoption by which we cry out "Abba! Father!"'*

This term of *'Abba, Father'* is a term denoting deep reverence for God, but also the cry of a child who reaches out to be picked up or embraced by a parent. This is God's heart cry rising up within us for His Spirit. A cry or longing for deep intimacy with His children. Since we know that we are made in His image, it is not a far-flung premise to understand that one's need of a soul-mate, a husband or wife, is actually a reflection of God's nature within us to experience deep intimacy.

As was stated in the previous chapter every human being

has two basic emotional, or heart needs; first a sense of significance. We need to know that to those in our immediate situation, such as family and close friends, we are of value to them. Secondly, we all need a sense of security. That is, we need a sense that our lives are going to be okay and that we are going to survive and even prosper in our souls. Fallen mankind has basically done its best to find ways to compensate for a sense of security and significance derived from the the Father's perfect love. For some that would be their income and material belongings. Their luxury houses, clothes, and cars, are sought after not so much for survival as for the sake of prestige. Jesus warned not to be as the Gentiles, or ungodly, who eagerly seek after these things. Others out of desperation or rejection might turn to drugs or some other fix as a form of compensation. That fix could be promiscuous or illicit sex, it could be notoriety in a certain area of expertise, it could be power in their industry or circle of friends. Many will become slaves to current social whims and attempt to gain popularity as a replacement for God's love. The bottom line, however, is that as created beings, especially created in the Triune God's image, we were created to have deep relationship with God. Any substitution for that relationship, while it may satisfy short term, is only a band-aid for a real poverty.

That poverty, which may seem deep with some and shallow with others, is an issue of the heart. It carries over into the emotions, but basically it is a heart issue. Therein is the problem for many Christians and leaders. Jesus did not come merely so that we could intellectually understand the truth. He came that we might experience, or have a living relationship, with the truth Himself. In Jesus' discourse against those who were persecuting Him in John, chapter 5, He makes the distinction between primarily an intellectual knowledge and an experiential knowledge of God. He states in verses 39 and 40:

'*You diligently study the Scriptures because you think that by them you possess eternal life. These are the scriptures that testify about me, yet you refuse to come to me to have life.'*

An experiential knowledge of God without an intellectual knowledge leaves one wide open for deception, because even Satan can appear as an angel of light. But the overwhelming problem Jesus was confronted with was a pharisaic approach to God which immediately discredited the unfamiliar and unknown.

Basically, what is in conflict is the difference between heart knowledge and head knowledge. Both are essential. Neither is complete in itself. A primary focus on experience can lead to a preoccupation with tangents if not actual deception or heresy. A primary intellectual knowledge of God can lead to legalism, a reliance on method and tradition, and a focus on outward appearances. Paul stated that he was not a minister of the law but of the Spirit.

Salvation in the fullest sense of the word means a lot more than escaping the fires of hell and living on streets of gold in heaven. In Matthew 5:48 where Jesus states, *'Be perfect, even as your heavenly Father is perfect,'* He is using the Greek word *'teleios'*. Basically, *'teleios'* means to be complete, including growth and moral character. In John 14:30 Jesus stated that the prince of this world, or Satan, had nothing on Him. Jesus was free to say this because He was complete, or perfect, in the will of the Father and wholeness of the Father. There were no hooks, open doors, or entanglements, by which Satan could manipulate Him.

Unfortunately none of us are nearly that whole, or perfect, as Jesus. But that is the goodness of the Kingdom of God. God, in the form of the Emmanuel, is here. His reign and love are available to all who seek Him. A trap for many Christians, however, can be that even though the basis of a relationship with God through the cross is restored, the relationship with God can be neglected for the **things** of God. Those things could be legalism, meaning a primary focus on outward behaviour. It could be ministry for God, but outside of the ongoing flow of intimacy with God. In

Matthew chapter 7, verses 21–23, Jesus warns that on the day of judgement there will be some locked out of His presence who have done a lot of ministry. Even ministry in His Name.

This is a critical warning for high visionary, goal-focused Christian leaders to take into account. It is easy to assume that because either correct doctrine is being taught, or legitimate healings, deliverances, and prophesies are being done, that it absolutely means a ministry or individual is in God's will. During the early part of the 1980s my wife and I were heading up an attempt to start a church in Southern California. The church met twice a week, one corporate meeting and for a period of time in two home groups. I was greatly perplexed as to why the church never grew to more than 30 people at its height. Many of the meetings were punctuated by strong prophesies over people's lives that were very encouraging. There were many meetings where correct words of knowledge and subsequent healings were happening. There would often be a strong dynamic of the Holy Spirit's presence. But after a year and a half not only was the church not growing but we were losing people who we could not afford to lose. I simply could not understand what was wrong. One week while at a pastor's conference and hearing a message about first and foremost seeking the Father and His will, I came into the realization that I had never really sensed God telling me to plant the church in the first place. As I began to pray into this the Lord overwhelmingly showed me that there was an anointing on the meetings because He had placed an anointing on my life. But that certainly did not mean I had a spiritual carte blanche to do whatever I liked even if the intentions were good intentions.

Those that Jesus talked of in Matthew 7 will have done things in His name; most probably by His Spirit. But from Balaam we learn that even a donkey can be anointed. Jesus stated that He would call those doing works of power but out of His will *'evil doers'*. These *'evil doers'* are in contrast to those who *'do the will of My Father'*. Whether Jesus meant cast out of heaven or His immediate presence in heaven is perhaps debatable, but either way this warning cannot be ignored. The gifts of God **are** given without repentance, Romans 11:29, but operating in the gifting, whatever it may be, does not necessarily mean being in the fullness of the Father's will. And therein lies the problem for potential spiritual abusers.

A leader can have a powerful anointing for leading, teaching, preaching, healing, prophecy, or evangelism. That leader can have good intentions and vision. But, that leader can have a multitude of hooks, or entanglements, from the enemy and either be ignorant of them or attempt to cover them up. If he, or she, is not first and foremost operating out of the wholeness and motivation of the Father's heart, no matter how great the anointing the ministry will be tainted, if not polluted. Jesus unequivocally pointed this out in Matthew 12:35:

> *'A good man out of the good treasure of the heart bringeth forth good things.'*

Proverbs 4:23 states:

> *'Above all else, guard your heart, for it is the wellspring of life.'*

When I was attempting to church plant in the early 1980s I was so sure I had to be in God's will. After all, wanting to evangelize and teach people about God were good intentions. But as I allowed the Holy Spirit to search my motives I began to find a number of issues at work in me besides the good intentions. David's song labeled as Psalm 139 is a song exalting the Lord for the thoroughness of His love for each of us. Towards the end of the psalm David fearlessly invites God to search his heart to see if he had any wrongful, or hurtful motives. David, according to 1 Chronicles 28, instructed his son Solomon to serve God with a whole heart because *'the Lord searches every heart and understands every motive behind the thoughts.'* Jeremiah states in Jeremiah 17:9:

'The heart is deceitful above all things and beyond cure. Who can understand it?'

The lessons I learned by inviting the Lord to sift my motives were foundational. I turned the church plant over to someone else, and began to focus on areas of ministry that I was not just gifted for, but specifically directed by the Father to do at that time. That does not mean that there have been no problems since then because warfare, trials, and sometimes frustration accompany all of us from time to time. But I began to really understand at that time the reality of what the Psalmist wrote in Psalm 127:

'Unless the Lord is the builder the labourers labour in vain.'

Since January of 1994 we have had well over 800,000[2] visitors to our church, the Toronto Airport Christian Fellowship. They have come because of the recent move of the Holy Spirit dubbed by the British press the 'Toronto Blessing'. At our church we have close to 300 trained ministry team members. These 300 ministry team people are mostly from our church, and some from other churches in the Toronto area that we have good relationship with. These are the people that night after night do the bulk of the actual ministry in praying for the visitors. Almost all of these team members have gone through training in various areas of ministry such as praying for the sick, praying for healing of past hurts, deliverance, words of knowledge, prophecy, etc. But the foundational teaching we take them through is a course designed to deal with issues in their own hearts. What we have found is that healthy people bless others with good blessings. As Jesus said, *'the good man speaks out of the abundance of the heart.'*

The opposite is also true; hurting people hurt others. For example, most child abusers were themselves abused as children. Despite their intentions to 'never do to their children what their parents did to them' they carry on the curse if their anger and bitterness are not released through the power of forgiveness and repentance. This is why, as leaders in Toronto Airport Christian Fellowship, we place such a priority on wholeness rather than merely gifting for our ministry team members as well as pastoral staff. Part of the fruit is that, although we are far from perfect, many visitors from all over the world have commented time and time again that what they received the most from our church was a deeper understanding of God's grace and love for His children.

It can be an easy trap for a Christian, especially for someone called to full-time ministry, to develop a warped view of the Holy Spirit and His gifts. A view in which the gifts of the Spirit are more valued than the relationship with the Spirit. One can arrive at the place of ministering in the power of the Holy Spirit but have no real priority for spending time in personal worship and prayer with the Lord. Likewise, a teacher can have a great intellectual appreciation for the Bible and theology but neglect the person of the Lord Jesus. As stated earlier one can be more in love with the truth about Jesus, than Jesus the Truth Himself. This is not only a potential danger towards one's own relationship with God. If a leader grows to the point of merely using the gifts of the Spirit it will cross over into how he or she values others.

Part of the beauty of the Psalm 139 is that it powerfully states God's inherent love for individuals:

> *'For you created my inmost being; you knit me together in my mother's womb. I praise you because I am fearfully and wonderfully made; your works are wonderful, I know that full well.'* (Psalm 139:13–14)

God loves people. Not just the big crowd or the masses, but He loves individuals. It is because of God's love for individuals, as opposed to just humanity, that He sent Jesus to die on the cross, and then fill us with His Spirit individually as we surrender our lives to Him. It is out of the ongoing revelation of God's heart for the lost and the hurting that those in church leadership should maintain their vision and cry for the lost and the hurt. Jesus often ministered out of compassion for the lost, the hungry, and the blind.

When a leader begins to use the gifts of the Spirit apart from intimacy with God it is often a very short step away from beginning to abuse individuals for the sake of the vision or program. The church people around that leader will be seen as tools or pawns that can be used and even viewed as expendable for the sake of the 'bigger picture'. Jesus pictured Himself as the good shepherd who would leave the ninety-nine to find the one lost sheep. Intimacy with the Holy Spirit is where the ongoing revelation of God's heart flows. It is out of the overflow of God's heart from our hearts that we grow to be as Jesus is: a lover of people, not only concerned about the big picture.

In the last chapter we briefly discussed Jesus' taking off His outer garments at the last supper in order to reveal His heart. He gave the disciples a final lesson before the crucifixion that He, being Lord, did not come to be served, but rather to serve. This is one of several occasions in the Bible that has to do with the taking on or off of clothes. Adam and Eve were naked and unashamed until they disobeyed God. Then they covered up. King Saul, in 1 Samuel, chapter 19, ended up taking his clothes off and prophesying naked for 24 hours when the Spirit of God came on him. David, when bringing the Ark of God into the city of David, took off his outer clothes and using a priest's jacket like a kilt, publicly leaped and danced with all of his might. Peter, in John 21, on understanding that it was Jesus on the shore, put on his outer clothing and jumped into the water to swim to Jesus. All of these stories have to do with the willingness to be transparent, or vulnerable, before God and man. David when rebuked by his wife for *'uncovering himself as one of the foolish ones'* responded that before God he would humble himself even more than that.

The one story of the group that is the least obvious is of Peter **putting on** clothes to swim to Jesus. We know that if one falls out of a boat, it is better to take off heavy outward garments as it's easier to swim and stay afloat without them pulling you down. But Peter here is doing the opposite. He had been stripped down to his shorts for working in the boat, but on learning that it was actually Jesus who had instructed them to throw the net out into deeper water began to 'get dressed'.

To understand this we need to remember what has just recently taken place. Jesus having been crucified is now very much alive and standing before them. Peter, however, was in a position of shame and guilt. He had denied Jesus three times the night of Jesus' arrest out of fear of association. He was overjoyed at Jesus' resurrection, but more than a little afraid of his own position. He had been the one who had said 'Lord, I am ready to go with you to prison and to death.' Peter formerly had been brash, confident, and perhaps proud of his faith and giftedness. The man now jumping into the water was rather humble and unsure of himself. In fact, he was no longer sure Jesus would even receive him in quite the old way, hence the covering up. He was now in a very similar position to Adam and Eve who made fig leaves for themselves to cover their nakedness before God and one another. Unlike, Adam and Eve, however, Peter did not hide from the Lord. Rather he ran, or swam to Him. Jesus, is His grace and compassion ministered healing to Peter. For each of the three denials He led Peter into a confession of love and commitment. What is of importance to us though is the fact that even though Peter was ashamed and covered up he still willingly sought the Lord's presence. He was not content to just stay in the boat even if they were being blessed by a great catch of fish from the Lord.

When King David was exposed by the prophet Nathan for his sin with Bathsheba and murdering Uriah her husband, he wrote in Psalm 51, verse 17:

> 'The sacrifices of God are a broken spirit; a broken and contrite heart, O God, you will not despise.'

David, in his heart, realized that what God wanted foremost

from him was not great outward sacrifices such as bulls and goats. It is so easy to end up in a 'performance orientated' relationship with God. We assume because we are making sacrifices for God and good things are happening that that in itself means we are walking in the fullness of God's love.

When we look at Peter leading up to the time of his denials of Jesus it seems that most probably, pride had strongly developed. He had been the one to hear from the Father that Jesus was the Messiah. Peter was the one who had the faith to get out of the boat and walk on water with Jesus. Peter was one of the three disciples allowed to see Jesus in His glory on the mount of transfiguration. His pride was in evidence when He told Jesus that He was not to go to Jerusalem and be arrested. And again, when he proclaimed, *'All others will deny you, but not me.'*

A friend of mine, Ron Allen, who has been in ministry for over 25 years, often says of Satan's tactics 'if the enemy can't get you through starving you with failure, he gets you by stampeding you with success.' The point being that it seems sometimes in our endeavour to serve God when success does come, if our hearts are not in a place of seeking God's heart, pride develops.

Pride is the original sin, even predating Adam and Eve. It was Satan's sin as he reflected on his beauty and glory and forgot that he was created by God. Adam and Eve were tempted by Satan's seduction to be 'as God'. To have enough knowledge to be in control of their own lives. God hates sin, but especially pride in His children. His hatred of pride stems from the fact that when a person, including a Christian, stands in pride there is no realization or longing for God's grace and provision. God is very much against the proud but gives grace to the humble.

When a person, including a Christian leader, is in a place of high regard for their own abilities outside of a thankful heart to God, pride can become predominant. As spiritual pride in the life of a Christian develops, there is less and less of a sense of constant need for God's grace, mercy, and leading. The fruit of that is less prayer time spent in seeking

God and waiting and ministering to Him. Part of the syndrome is a growing devaluation of those in the family of God who cannot produce. A disdain can develop for those who are not as anointed or on the cutting edge. Soon those underneath us in authority are seen as tools, or pawns, to help facilitate 'our ministries' rather than the ministry of Jesus. Soon we are deriving our identities from our work for Christ, rather than our relationship with Him. We become 'the pastor', or 'the anointed' evangelist or teacher. All others are of secondary importance.

When pride is allowed to go unchecked, it puts up barriers between our hearts and intimacy with God. As intimacy grows less with God, it is easy for a hardness, or callousness to develop towards others of seemingly less importance in 'the big picture'. Paul addresses the syndrome of taking a utilitarian view of people in 1 Corinthians, chapter 12. He wrote in verses 22 and 23:

> *'On the contrary, those parts of the body that seem to be weaker are indispensable, and the parts that we think are less honorable we treat with special honor. And the parts that are unpresentable are treated with special modesty.'*

He metaphorically pictured those in the family of God that don't seem as 'valuable' like certain areas of the human body that we treasure and protect.

God's love for the individual is intrinsic. There is a God-given dignity and value to each human being regardless of their calling, gifting, or fruitfulness. It was for this reason that Jesus came and died on a cross – a physician for those who were sick and broken instead for those who are well, a deliverer for the captives rather than for the free. There is no human on the face of the earth that is not of great value to God. Unfortunately, Darwinism, or survival of the fittest, has had a big impact not only on the world cultures but also on some of the church. It is all too easy in high vision, goal-oriented churches to value only those who can help the leadership achieve their goals. The opposite side of the pendulum is equally deplorable; a disregard for vision, anointing, and callings for the sake of making everyone comfortable in the big, sagging bed of mediocrity. In the middle of that pendulum is the place where church leadership can be committed to raising up workers according to their giftings and callings, but not lose sight of God's goal; to heal the broken, set the captives free, befriend and comfort the lonely, and give hope to the hopeless. The church is not only to be an army but also a hospital.

The key to maintaining that balance is always intimacy with God. Intimacy with God, on an ongoing basis brings about fruit in several areas. In primarily just having good Bible knowledge, or theology, it is easy to get a fat head, as Paul warned of in 1 Corinthians 8:1. A focus on our good works and accomplishments for Christ can also lead to pride. But, having a primary focus on seeking God's face means having both in balance. We read and study the Bible because we want to know Christ and be more like Him. We serve Him with our time, energy, and money because we want to glorify Him, not to earn positions or titles. When we pray not just for answers to our requests, but also to worship Him we are brought to our knees in the deepening revelation of His glory and sovereignty. As we meet with Him in prayer and worship, we are humbled by the growing revelation of our undeservedness of His great love. As we spend time with Him we are changed by the revelation of Himself. As the Apostle Paul put it we are to go 'from glory to glory' rather than teaching to teaching or success to success.

There are two occasions where Peter got 'out of the boat'. Both were in response to Jesus' presence, but with very different goals. The first was in the excitement of seeing Jesus do the impossible. Peter greatly wanted to join in the fun. That is a picture of God's heart for us – to join in the fun and do the impossible no matter what our situation. But the second time, when Jesus stood on the shore, was a picture of Peter being desperate out of humility for His love and forgiveness. This is also very much the Father's heart for us.

To 'get out of the boat' means being willing to forsake the status quo as well as our personal comfort zones. It means to be so desperate for Jesus, that we are not concerned with merely 'maintaining'. The prophet Habakkuk said when speaking on waiting for the Lord:

> *'As for the proud one, his heart is not right within him.'*
> (Habakkuk 2:4, NAS)

When Peter humbled himself and came to the Lord Jesus in John 21 he found forgiveness, healing, and a commissioning. God is longing for us to trust His heart and compassion to the extent, that rather than covering up as Adam and Eve did, we run to Him. We see the Father's heart so clearly in the parable of the prodigal son. As the son came with fear and trepidation towards the family property the father, seeing him across the fields, went running to him to lovingly embrace his son.

God is wanting to release power and authority to the church for the purpose of revival and a great harvest. The key to entering in is more than just faith and revelation. We need to come to the place that Peter was at; to run to Christ not only to 'join the fun', but out of humility to seek His healing love. Often our prayers are 'more power, more anointing'. We need to come to the place of 'Oh God, search my heart, so I may be more like You and less myself!' There is a major Pentecost upon the church in the late 1990s. But the key is, as Isaiah put it:

> *'This is the one I esteem: he who is humble and contrite in spirit, and trembles at my word.'* (Isaiah 66:2)

Notes

1. James 1:22.
2. A very conservative estimate as of December 1996.

Chapter 5

Ministering with Transparency – The Jesus Style

'He who conceals his trangressions will not prosper, But he who confesses, and forsakes them will find compassion.'
(Proverbs 28:13)

In the last chapter we looked briefly at the motivation for Peter jumping into the water and swimming towards Jesus. In this chapter I would like to examine more fully what it means to minister out of wholeness and the effect it has on those we minister to.

As quoted in the last chapter, Jesus in John 14:30, stated that the prince of this world, Satan, was coming but that he (Satan) had nothing on Jesus. He then said in verse 31:

'... the world must learn that I love the Father and that I do exactly what my Father has commanded me.'

Jesus was the first person on earth to ever live a life of complete submission to the Father. If He had done any less He would have disqualified Himself from being the perfect lamb of God without blemish. It is important in studying abuse of authority that we understand why Jesus lived the life He did. Jesus' love for the Father was not just the motivation for what He did, but it was the grid or framework in which He thought, moved, and lived.

Jesus was not only from the Father. He, the Word, was with God in the beginning and all things came into being by Him, according to John 1. This is significant, in that everything created has been made by the Son who loved pleasing the Father. Everything that has been created by Him, including humanity was designed out of this flow of love. It has always been God's fullest intent that we too, should live and flourish in the same environment of His love. Anything less falls short of God's will for our lives. God is love, as John stated in the book of 1 John. Divine love is, or was and shall be again, the ethos of the universe. The freedom of the cross cannot be totally experienced, until the Son's love for the Father is understood.

The complete depths of that love is beyond what we can ever fully comprehend in this realm. As it says in Psalm 145:3, *'His glory is unsearchable!'* Be that as it may, Jesus did say that He came that we might have life and experience it in abundance. In short, He came to restore us to that place of knowing the Father in intimacy. The garden of Eden is lost to humanity, at least until the return of the Lord. But the grace to know the Father has been restored by the cross. The cross itself is the very picture of the Father's love for us. Jesus was sent to explain the Father and then ultimately to die on the cross as the full measure of the Father's heart. This is why the Apostle Paul could say with great confidence, that:

> *'He who did not spare his own Son, but gave him up for us all – how will he not also, along with him, graciously give us all things?'*

Jesus is the Word, the Logos, the Father explained. He said to Philip that he who had seen Jesus had seen the Father.

The 20th-century, western-world lifestyle is one rampant with rejection and fragmentation. Friends, mates, and loyalties are quickly discarded when a new and better situation comes along. It can be very difficult for us to conceptualize the bond of love that existed between Jesus and the Father. We often don't see beyond the 'do's and don'ts', the 'rights and wrongs' when we look at the life and words of Jesus because we are preconditioned against unconditional love and acceptance. Jesus did not do what He did out of fear of the Father's wrath or displeasure. It was His love for the Father and the desire to please Him in all things. *'My will is to do the will of the One who sent Me,'* He stated. But Jesus' actions did not stem from attempting to prove something to the Father. Because He was one in essence with the Father love, the essence of God permeated all of Jesus' being, thoughts, and deeds. He knew fully where He had come from and to where He was returning – the right hand of a loving Father.

Because Jesus was so filled with the Spirit and knowledge of the Father's love, all He **could** want to do was please the Father. That is not to say that temptation was not real for Him, because it was. But He knew that His true food, His true joy was being one with the Father. His heart and will for us is nothing short of the same type of intimacy. He prayed for it in John 17, verses 21–22, that just as He was in the Father and the Father in Him, that we could, also be in unity in Him.

Unity is one of the real keys to realizing the fullness of what the Lord has for the body of Christ. In Psalm 133 we read:

> *'How good and pleasant it is for brothers to dwell together in unity! It is like the precious oil upon the head, coming down upon the beard, even Aaron's beard, coming down upon the edge of his robes. It is like the dew of Hermon coming down upon the mountains of Zion. For there the* LORD *commanded the blessing – life forever.'* (NAS)

The place where God has **commanded** blessings to flow is in a place where brothers are dwelling together in unity.

Unity is one of the primary prophetic words that the Holy

Spirit is speaking to the body of Christ. Partially, for the purpose of city-wide revivals being birthed. But beyond that is the bigger event of the *parousia* – the return of Jesus for His bride! But unfortunately, some of the teaching regarding the importance of unity has to do with religious conformity rather than relationship. The creativity of God demands that His love be expressed through the church not only in a wide variety of ways, but also through a wide variety of people. The Holy Spirit brings freedom of creativity, while the spirit of religion breeds fear which, in turn, demands conformity. An outward moulding of round pegs into square holes is not what the Bible means by unity. In God's liberty there is freedom for a great variety of personality and expression. The unity God demands is a deep regard and caring for one another. Not despite our outward differences, but in the appreciation and dovetailing of our strengths and weaknesses. Biblical unity calls for the preferring and esteeming of one another based on God's intrinsic value of each person in the Body of Christ.

As discussed earlier in the book the last lesson that Jesus chose to give His disciples prior to the crucifixion, was a lesson in transparency and love. He took off His outward garments, and using a towel wrapped around His waist, He washed the feet of the disciples. This would normally be the job of the lowliest of servants. He responded to the surprise and chagrin of the disciples by saying that if this is how He, the Master, acted towards them, so they ought to act towards one another. One of the keys to understanding this lesson is in the fact that He removed His outer clothing, signifying a willingness to be transparent before God and man.

In our western culture sociologists have observed what is called 'Rules of Disclosure'. Rules of Disclosure describe the tendencies natural to all of us regarding personal communication. Usually we do not feel comfortable disclosing personal feelings and thoughts much deeper than the individual or group with us is willing to reciprocate. We often feel highly uncomfortable even listening to someone else's personal state if we are not able to reciprocate. This is one of the reason for the popularity of bars. Once the alcohol is flowing inhibitions come down and everyone is a friend.

This tendency to avoid disclosure goes all the way back to the garden of Eden. A distrust in God's mercy and compassion resulted in the great cover up by Adam and Eve. Since that time most of us are more comfortable hiding behind facades or masks. The facade can be that of an athlete, a scholar, a lawyer, or mechanic, or a minister. That is to say, we derive our security and significance in part from our projected image. In North America, there is the phenomena that many business and professional people begin to suffer a deterioration in health soon after retirement. This is at least partially due to feeling that because there is no reason to carry on wearing their masks any more, their purpose in life is over. However, we can allow our masks to so completely dominate our lives that our God-given uniqueness is swallowed up by conformity.

Where I grew up in Southern California, in high school, at ages 13–17 or 18, virtually everyone derived their identity through their performance. They were a 'jock' if they majored in sports. They were an 'egghead' if they got straight A's. They were a 'loadee' if they focused on doing drugs, or a surfer, or skate boarder, and so on. You were either in a scene or you just did not belong. Many refused to have any friendships outside of their scene or group. The underlying problem, however, was that one was really not accepted because of who they were. Rather, they were accepted by their appearance or performance. It was the rare individual who was happy in and of himself. The same tendency can be true for many Christians. Despite Paul's warning about saying 'I am of Paul, or I am of Apollos, or I follow Cephas' that is often what we do. We wear Baptist clothes, or Pentecostal clothes, or Anglican clothes. Sometimes this is literally true. You can visit some churches and everyone tends to dress, style their hair, and speak alike. But the main point here is not really about outward appearances, but the ability to be **real**.

In a performance-based church, as opposed to a relationship-based church, one's value and significance come from the outward performance. Therein lies the problem. Many years ago while preaching in a church in Mexico City, I made the statement that no one is perfect except for God. I went on to point out that even a pastor, although he might be mature and gifted, was not perfect in measuring up to Christ's holiness. The translator, I found out later from bilingual friends with me, did not translate me fully at that point, for fear that people would think of himself, the pastor, as being less than perfect. This is obviously an extreme example of a leader afraid to be real. The average Christian, or leader, behind a facade is not nearly this blatant, but it can be far more serious because of the subtlety.

To discuss leaders and facades it is probably helpful to look at a clear biblical illustration. In the story of the the young shepherd boy David going out to fight the giant Goliath, King Saul advised David to wear his armour. David put on the armour but then complained to Saul: *'I can not go with these, for I have not tested them.'* David then took off the clothes, helmet, and armour. In today's language David would have said, 'This isn't me.' Just as God had been with David when he had killed the lion and the bear while protecting his father's sheep, David knew that God would be with him in fighting this enemy of God's sheep. He realized his God-given abilities and anointing were not conditional in fighting with another's weapons or wearing another's clothes.

One of the most awesome freedoms the cross brings is that we can walk with Christ constantly by His Holy Spirit. One of the names of Jesus reflects this: the Emmanuel – the God who is with us. Jesus told His disciples that He would never leave them nor forsake them. When a person surrenders his or her life to Jesus they become born again by the Spirit of God coming to dwell within them. They receive 'the Spirit of adoption' by which they become the sons and daughters of God. Whatever gifts or anointing God gives us is within us. The natural abilities God gives us are unique to us as individuals made wonderfully and fearfully even while in our mother's womb (Psalm 139:13–14). The supernatural gifts God gives us are within us due to the indwelling of the Holy Spirit. Hence, the gifts, whether natural or supernatural, are in us not in a form or a model to be copied from someone else.

Unfortunately, one of the primary characteristics of toxic faith type churches is conformity to the leader's style and person. The opposite is also true – there is a devaluation of the God-given uniqueness of the individual. This phenomena in social terms is called 'Cult of Personality'. It is what takes place in society or a group of people where a leader is so mesmerizing and controlling that most individuals deny their own uniqueness for the sake of emulating their leader in every way possible. Leaders are to be honored, no doubt, but not to the point where we are in denial of who we are as individuals. When the Apostle Paul said in 1 Corinthians 11:1, *'Follow my example, as I follow the example of Christ,'* he was not saying style yourself after me, but **you too** be an imitator of Christ.

As I pointed out in the beginning of the book, often people who are abused by leaders are inadvertently asking for it. The people of the prophet Samuel's day wanted a king they could look at and talk to like the other nations. So it is with many Christians today. A committed, serious, Christian can become so wrapped up in building the empire of a pastor or leader that they lose sight of seeking first the Kingdom of God. Their prayer life can end up devoid of worship and person-to-person communication with God. Instead of worshipping the Father in Spirit and in Truth we can easily place much of our trust and focus on a man (or woman). In effect, we are setting ourselves up for a fall. Jesus said to the religious leaders of His time:

> *'How can you believe if you accept praise from one another, yet make no effort to obtain the praise that comes from the only God?'* (John 5:44)

Of all the people who have ever served God, few have ever

moved in an anointing such as Elijah did. To this day he is one of the great heroes of the Hebrew people. A place is still set for him at the table when celebrating the Passover meal. It was Elijah, along with Moses, who stood in glory on the mount of Transfiguration with Jesus in Matthew 17. It was his spirit, or anointing that was in John the Baptist. But concerning Elijah, James said this: he *'was a man with a nature like ours.'* That means that even though he was mightily used by God he fell short of God's standards of holiness.

One of the amazing things about the Bible is that God does not leave out the flaws, warts, and spiritual burps of His anointed ones. We can read of Elijah running out of fear from Queen Jezebel. One day he is calling down fire from heaven and killing the false priests and prophets of Baal, the next he is controlled by fear. We read about David radically in love with God and zealously killing God's enemies. Then we read of the great man of God committing adultery and premeditated murder. We read of Peter with great faith walking on water one moment and the next almost sinking out of fear of the waves. Gideon was used powerfully by God to lead Israel out of bondage to the Midianites, but years later he led Israel into harlotry with false worship (see Judges 8:22–28). These stories of the failures in faith, courage, and morals by God's leaders are definitely not in the Bible by accident. They are there for two basic reasons. First God wants us to realize that the battle and the glory belong to Him. As Zechariah said: *'not by might, not by power, but by My Spirit says the Lord.'* Secondly, and equally as important, God wants us to know that He does not despise our humanity. Neither is He embarrassed by it. In fact, He loves our humanity. He hates sin because sin is rebellion against Him and sin brings about destruction. But, He loves sinners. He loves hurt, broken, and imperfect people.

One of the primary ways in which God glorifies Himself is by working through imperfect, and often weak, people. In becoming born again, adopted into God's family, we are

77

called to be the peace-makers, or ambassadors on behalf of Christ. We are automatically enrolled into God's army to make war against the kingdom of Satan, the prince of this world. But all too often, serious, well-meaning, committed Christians fall into the trap of seeing themselves as a second-class saints because of the division many leaders establish between themselves and the people.

Psalm 8, verse 2 reads:

'From the lips of children and infants you have ordained praise because of your enemies, to silence the foe and the avenger.'

In the process of bringing about the downfall of Satan God is deeply humbling him by using very weak vessels. Satan in his fall from glory came to earth in an attempt to completely corrupt humanity, created in God's image. Man in comparison to angelic beings is very weak and fragile. Satan, seemingly, found Adam and Eve, our father and mother figures, an easy target and was able to drive a definite wedge between man and God. What Satan was ignorant of, was God's divine plan to rescue fallen humanity by His only begotten Son becoming human Himself. In so doing, those who respond to Christ, become the adopted sons and daughters of God who are called to be Christians or 'little Christs'. As it says in Ephesians 2:10:

'For we are God's workmanship, created in Christ Jesus to do good works, which God prepared in advance for us to do.'

Some of the most powerful creative miracles I have personally witnessed the Lord do have happened at times when I 'felt' very little faith or confidence that one would happen. One of the times I will never forget concerns a little boy of about seven years old with a club foot. He had to use specially made shoes. He could walk okay, but whenever he tried to run and play with the other kids he would fall down. His mother brought him to me for prayer as I was leaving the last night of a series of meetings. I was tired from three or four hours of ministry that night and the previous two nights. I was so drained I felt very little faith that a healing would happen. But right before my eyes as I was more or less going through the motions, I could see his muscles and bones changing shape under the skin. The whole healing process lasted less than 10 seconds. To my amazement he then proceeded to start running all around the interior of the church. His mother was enthusiastically jumping up and down out of sheer joy. I was thinking: 'wait, come back! I have not finished my prayer yet.' This healing helped me more fully grasp Paul's great confession that *'God's strength was perfected in his* (Paul's) *weakness.'*

When we, as leaders or ministers, humble ourselves to the point of transparency and vulnerability before those we are ministering to we give a message that more than words alone can convey. That is, we become a living letter, or testimony of God's grace. In all of the letters of the Bible written by the apostle Paul, he greets the churches with the blessing of *'Grace and peace to you from God our Father and the Lord Jesus Christ.'* In his letters to Timothy, he adds 'mercy' to the blessing. Paul ministered in, and out of, a tremendous ongoing revelation of God's grace. His proclamation was that *'I know that nothing good lives in me, that is, in my sinful nature'* (Romans 7:18). He was deeply conscious not only of his former life of persecuting the church, but that he continually fell short of God's standards. He continued on in verses 18 and 19:

> *'For I have the desire to do what is good, but I cannot carry it out. For what I do is not the good I want to do; no, the evil I do not want to do – this I keep on doing.'*

Jesus, living in a deep flow of the Father's perfect love for Him was not afraid to be vulnerable before His disciples. He says in John 12, verse 27, *'Now is my soul troubled.'* In His intense time of prayer in the garden of Gethsemane He was not afraid to tell Peter, James, and John that He needed their prayers. At the last supper, which we have already looked at, Jesus was not afraid of taking the place of a lowly servant – washing the disciples' feet with His own garments and being partially naked before them. The removal of His outer garments was just as significant to the story as the act of washing their feet was. He was not just instructing the disciples to minister one to another, but to be **vulnerable and transparent** with one another.

The age-old distinction of cleric and laity, is actually antibiblical in its connotations. We are all called to be priests in seeking and serving the Lord Jesus. But, it is true that not all are called to serve in the capacity of leadership, or fourfold ministry. Be that as it may however, too many leaders have established barriers between themselves and the church that lead to devaluation and sometimes abuse. Unfortunately, the worst barrier is probably spiritual pride. When we see Jesus in the gospels, He lived not only as the only begotten Son of God but also very much as a man of the people. He was not afraid to socialize with thieves and prostitutes. He took delight in their humanness. The thieves, beggars, outcasts, and prostitutes had no masks of religious pride or outward respectability to hide behind. It was natural for Jesus to find their company more real than many of the leaders. In fact, according to Matthew 21:31 Jesus told the chief priest and the elders at the Temple, that some prostitutes and tax gatherers were entering the Kingdom of God before them.

A common assumption is that a leader is qualified to be a leader because of deeper maturity and holiness. Without basic biblical maturity, such as Paul outlined to Timothy and Titus, an elder can not really function as an elder. However – and this is a big however – leaders, no matter how strongly anointed are still human beings. Their qualification is the calling and gifting. The maturity and integrity allows them to walk in the fullness of the gifting, but gifts, callings, and anointing from the Holy Spirit can never be earned or bought; they are gifts or expressions of God's priceless love in our midst. And this why it is essential that we do not despise our humanity. God is glorified by using humans, not despite our weaknesses, but with joy and grace as He demonstrates His nature, or grace in the midst of our weakness. This was Paul's boast: *'God's strength is perfected in My weakness.'* It is important to realize in using the term 'weakness' I do not mean practising sin. I am not prescribing a 'cheap grace' where we are free to sin since God will forgive us anyway. On the contrary, the final definition of grace is not that we are free to do what we want, but that we are free in Christ, by the power of the Holy Spirit to do what the Father wants us to do.

What I am saying, can be summarized by a saying of John Arnott, senior pastor of Toronto Airport Christian Fellowship:

'God loves us just the way we are, but He loves us too much to leave us that way.'

We are completely acceptable to God **right now** because of the wonder of the cross. This is our testimony! Right now, just as we are, if we have surrendered our lives to Christ we are the adopted sons and daughters of God. However, all of us, without exception, are in the continuing process of sanctification and consecration. Sanctification being the ongoing work of the Holy Sprit within us and consecration being the ongoing process of surrender and daily picking up our cross to follow Christ. Justification is what took place at the cross.

When ministry that will bear eternal fruit takes place it is because of the grace of God's power, love, and anointing on our lives. We must stand before the people of God, and the world, and not trust or promote our own abilities. Like the Psalmist sang in Psalm 20:7:

'Some trust in chariots and some in horses, but we trust in the name of the LORD our God.'

We can be real with people. In fact, we can choose to be vulnerable to the point where we are making certain to the people that we, like Elijah, have the same nature as they. Like Paul, we can say, *'If I must boast, I will boast of the things that show my weakness.'*

When a leader without humility stands before the church continually posturing in his abilities and strengths he, or she, is giving a very strong message to the church. That message may not be intended, but it is real none the less. The message is that as soon as you are as mature, strong, and as gifted as I 'then God can use you'. This unspoken message that continually confronts the church helps to perpetuate the 'one man show' style of ministry. Instead of understanding Paul's instructions for Apostles, Prophets, Evangelists, and Pastor/Teachers to build up and equip the church to do ministry, many leaders see the 'sheep' as merely there to support their ministry. We will discuss that view later on in the book.

I am not saying that leaders should use the pulpit to focus continually on their faults and shortcomings. That, too, would be pride, only inverted. That would continue to be a focus on self rather than the Lord. Neither am I saying to confess shortcomings indiscriminately. I believe that just as bringing problems into the light is necessary, so it is important to use wisdom as to when and where we do so. James' instruction to confess our sins *'one to another,'* to a degree, implies your peers. Deep moral failings and other serious sins do, however, call for public repentance from leaders with public visibility.

In the context in which Jesus instructed the disciples to wash one another's feet He was speaking to the twelve alone. That is not to say we should not be a servant to all if possible. The point is that in-depth relationships are vital, but you cannot have deep friendships with everyone. There needs to be constants of relationships among peers where equity of trust and love can be developed.

When I speak of transparency, I mean that we are seeking to be in the position of continually directing the eyes and ears of the flock to the person of Jesus and not to ourselves. A healthy leader is one who is overjoyed by God's love, not the accolades of man. When a leader can be vulnerable before his church and say, yes God uses me, but it is totally His grace; because I am just like you, that is a sign of wholeness. It is at that point, that a leader can truly lead people into Christ-like lifestyles. When we let the people know that we also deal with trials, temptations, and frustration they can realize God can also anoint and work through their lives as well. They do not need to wait until they reach some unattainable state of near perfection.

Leaders need to express to the church that they too are going through the ongoing process of consecration and sanctification. When a leader stands behind a facade of perfection the church is always made to feel as just a little less spiritual than their leaders. In the last 15 years of international ministry all over the world I have met literally thousands of pastors. I have not met one, whether leading a big church or a little one that is not still dealing with issues in their life. The only difference between professional ministers and laity is the calling. And again, it needs to be thoroughly understood, that calling is a grace from the Lord, not something a leader can earn.

The great fear all of us have, which is an inheritance from our father and mother Adam and Eve, is the tendency to cover up our problems out of fear of rejection. We are constantly afraid that if people actually see us for who we are they will reject us, leave the church, quit supporting us, etc. Often, if not most of the time however, when we choose to be real or vulnerable, we will find that a response of love and even respect is evoked. People often respond 'Hey, this person is real. This is someone I can relate to. This is someone I can emulate. If my pastor can ask for prayer and encouragement, than maybe there's hope for me too.'

Obviously, I am not speaking here about serious sins such as gross immorality. But even in those severe cases that call for at least a season away from ministry for the sake of restoration, we find that when genuine forgiveness is asked for from the church usually love, sympathy, and help are genuinely offered in return. As I outlined in the first chapter, in the scenario of the young pastor trapped in his hurts, when little sins are not brought into the light the enemy will wreak havoc to the point where ministries, families, and churches are devastated. With a pastor, adultery usually does not happen overnight. The process is usually a long-term sliding deeper and deeper into bondage because of fear of rejection.

In the beginning of this chapter, we looked at Jesus' style of ministry being one of transparency. He was free to be real, because He lived in the constancy of the Father's perfect love. In 1 John 4:18, we read:

> *'There is no fear in love. But perfect love drives out fear, because fear has to do with punishment. The one who fears is not made perfect in love.'*

The word in the Greek used here for 'perfect' is *'teleios'*. The full meaning is to be whole, or complete in growth. Jesus was the first human to fully obey the Father and He was also the first complete or whole human in intimacy with the Father. He was, of course, fully God. But, we cannot truly comprehend the ministry of Jesus without completely taking into account the reality of His humanness.

In Hebrews chapter 4, verses 15 and 16 say this about Jesus:

> *'For we do not have a high priest who is unable to sympathize with our weaknesses, but we have one who has been tempted in every way, just as we are – yet was without sin. Let us then approach the throne of grace with confidence, so that we may receive mercy and find grace to help us in our time of need.'*

The writer of Hebrews is saying that we can have complete hope in all of our weakness because of the grace of God. Our high priest, Jesus, being fully human, as well as fully God, went through the same trials and temptations common to us. He fully understands and sympathizes with us. The good news of the cross is that payment has been made in full for all of our sins. We are free to receive grace – undeserved love, strength, peace, joy, self-control – not because we deserve it but because of the nature of God. The Bible says that God is against the proud, but gives grace to the humble. So much of the time when we stand in a posture of pride and/or denial we are in fact pushing away the help and healing the Spirit wants to extend to us.

To say we are humble before the Lord, but to stand in pride before the church is really a complete contradiction. The church, no matter how immature at this point, is the body of Christ because of the infilling of the Holy Spirit. To confess one's short comings to God, alone in the prayer closet, but to stand in a posture of perfection in front of God's people does not work. Again, I am not saying that leaders should indiscriminately share their sins. Neither should the pulpit be used for a constant 'show and tell' time. But leaders need to be real or else the barriers are real as well. Not only will Paul's directive for leaders to train and equip the church be short-circuited but Jesus' prayer to the Father – *'May they be one'* – will not take place.

When David instructed his son Solomon about building the temple for the Lord, He shared a prophecy God had given him regarding Solomon:

> *'He said to me: "Solomon your son is the one who will build my house and my courts, for I have chosen him to be my son, and I will be his father."'* (1 Chronicles 28:6)

David obviously loved Solomon, his son from Bathsheba, after the baby from adultery died. He was the one redeemed from the relationship. But God gave him a revelation that this son would have a very special father/son relationship with God Himself. God was saying this in the context of building the temple for the Lord. David continued in his prophecy concerning Solomon:

'[you] *shall be a man of rest; and I will give him rest from all his enemies on every side; for his name shall be Solomon, and I will give peace and quiet to Israel in his days.'*

This is one of the chief characteristics of maturity for a son of God – to be a man, or woman, of peace with peace dominating our relationships. But where there is not wholeness or *teleios* in our hearts, there is fear of punishment and rejection and the ensuing tendency to cover up and hide.

Jesus' driving motivation, His ethos, and banner was the Father's heart. His nourishment was doing the will of the Father. When a Christian leader is not doing what he does for the prize of pleasing the Father, that means he is being nourished by something else. Perhaps outward success by the size of the church or ministry, or perhaps the accolade of others. Jesus warned:

'Be careful not to do your "acts of righteousness" before men, to be seen by them. If you do, you will have no reward from your Father in heaven.'

Because of the fear of rejection so prevalent in our culture today there is a great danger for many Christians of being addicted to outward success in the eyes of man. Addicted to the degree that we see God's sons and daughters, purchased by the blood of the Lamb, as mere tools or resources. Addicted to the degree that we can be destroying the very people that God has called us to give our lives to.

We, as leaders or ministers are like Solomon called to build a temple to the Lord. Not temples of stone, but *'living stones being built up as a spiritual house for a holy priesthood.'* A temple that is in line with the chief cornerstone, Jesus Christ. But like Solomon, and like Jesus, we are not going to reach the fullness of our callings without first being sons to the Father, and secondly being the sons of God who are peacemakers and men of peace. We must adopt the

86

attitude of Jesus who did not regard His equality with God something to be grasped, but Who emptied Himself and took the form of a bondservant. We must be willing to take off our outer garments and serve people in humility. Not hiding behind masks of professionalism, but as brothers dwelling together in unity.

One of the most fearless prayers contained in the Bible is David's cry for healing in Psalm 139, verses 23–34:

> *'Search me, O God, and know my heart; test me and know my anxious thoughts. See if there is any offensive way in me, and lead me in the way everlasting.'*

David's heart knowledge of God's heart was so thorough, that even though he feared the Lord (see Psalm 64:9), he knew beyond a shadow of a doubt that God is a God of great mercy and compassion. David prayed in Psalm 86:15:

> *'But thou, O Lord, art a God full of compassion, and gracious, long-suffering, and plenteous in mercy and truth.'*

David out of his heart-knowledge of God dared to bring his hurts, sins, and shortcomings before the Father. He knew that rather than receiving punishment or wrath he would receive help, mercy, and grace. This is the story of David's life. A man who at times achieved greatness, but a man who had serious flaws. His strength however, and the reason God chose him over King Saul was that he had a heart burning after God.

Perhaps the most telling story about David's character is when his son Absalom raised up rebellion in the land against David. Rather than fight to his last breath in order to hang on to his position, he walked away so that Absalom would not bring destruction to the people of Jerusalem (2 Samuel 15:14). Like Jesus, David's trust was not in position or power but in God's mercy, compassion, and sovereignty. As it states in Psalm 75, verses 6–7:

> *'No one from the east or the west or from the desert can exalt a man. But it is God who judges: He brings one down, he exalts another.'*

David had an unfailing trust in God's heart for him. Quite often when trouble comes to us, our tendency is to strike out in defence, or try to make happen what we think is best. And often when we do so, even though we may think we are helping God, we can actually be responding out of a lack of faith in Him. Trials, problems, and even hurts do not come **despite** God's love for us. They come **with** God's permission for the sake of pruning and raising up our shortcomings, hurts, and vulnerabilities. The Father in His compassion allows these things because He is so deeply committed to us really being a living reflection of His Son Jesus.

When we are in a place of grasping and fighting for position, power, and prestige we often hinder the very healing that God is longing to do in our lives. I am not saying that leaders should give away authority to every wolf in sheep's clothing that comes along. But too much of the time, the eyes of our hearts are tainted by fear and envy. In that situation, it can be impossible to correctly assess the motives of other's hearts. When we begin to strive to hang on to 'what's ours' often a whirlwind of tension, striving, and distrust is released into the body of Christ.

The key is always trusting in God's goodness and love. This was the constant environment Jesus walked in. Satan had nothing on Him. There were no hooks the world or Satan had in Him by which He could be manipulated out of fully following the Father's will. Even if that meant losing many of His followers, or death by the hands of the people He had created. Isaiah 30:15 says:

> *'In repentance and rest is your salvation, in quietness and trust is your strength, but you would have none of it.'*

This formula for coming into the Father's will is just the opposite of our natural tendencies to strive and lash out.

If we can learn to start growing in a child-like relationship of trust in the Father's goodness we can begin to flow in real *koinonia* with the body of Christ – we can begin to relate as brothers rather than behind masks of professionalism. The fact that some brothers are called to be leaders and father figures does not take away from the fact that we are still brothers and called to esteem one another. The place of commanded blessing, where God's favour flows is when we are in relationships of preferring one another and building one another up to the full stature of maturity in Christ Jesus. Not mere looking after our own interests, but having Christ's attitude of selflessness towards each other.

And if we can learn to be brothers we can then grow to be true father figures within the Church. Paul said:

'You have ten thousand teachers but few fathers.'

Chapter 6

Who's on the Throne – Saul or David?

No biblical study of spiritual abuse would be complete without a contrast between the first two kings of Israel. In fact, one of the greatest books possibly ever written on the correct use of authority is *The Tale of Three Kings* by Gene Edwards. The book is a sketch of the tensions between first Saul and David, and then David and his son Absalom. What Gene brings out so beautifully is that David's best came out of a place of brokenness and humility.

The first king of Israel, Saul, was not chosen by God because he was a true reflection of God. Rather, he was chosen as a true representative of the people of Israel at that time. In some ways Saul **was** the best of Israel. He was a head taller than anyone else in Israel and there was not a more handsome man to be found in the land. Saul was a good warrior, and he knew how to perform religious offerings. Samuel said to Israel at, Mizpah:

> *'Do you see him whom the Lord has chosen? Surely there is not one like him among all the people.'*

In short he was probably to many the perfect king from an outward perspective. On occasions he was anointed by the Holy Spirit to both prophesy and to lead Israel courageously into battle.

Saul however, had a serious flaw for a leader – his heart was not captivated by God. When the prophet Samuel rebuked King Saul in 1 Samuel 13 verse 14, he said:

> *'But now your kingdom will not endure; the LORD has sought out a man after his own heart and appointed him leader.'*

The contrast between these two leaders is not unlike the differences between apathy in the contemporary church and the call today by the Holy Spirit to return to our first love of Jesus.

To say that Saul did not believe in God would be wrong. To say that he never looked to God for help would also be wrong. To say that he did not love God, to a degree, would be wrong too. Samuel, who lived a life of intense love for God and His people deeply grieved over God's rejection of Saul. Saul did have his good and strong points. But David, in contrast to Saul, did not merely believe in God or hope in God, but he lived for God with a radical passion.

Before we look at the defects in Saul, it would be helpful to look at one or two things that point to his good side. Often, part of the confusion experienced by many going through spiritual abuse is the fact that the leader is anointed and called by God. Often that leader has, in a sense, a heart of gold, and is an extremely nice guy. An ongoing conflict between two people is seldom a black and white scenario. This is part of the great dilemma concerning abusive leaders. They are usually not bad people, but do have their strong points and good sides. Saul was no different.

Briefly, let's look at two responses from Saul that effectively show his strengths. These are in the story of Saul leading a very successful rescue of the people of Jabesh from the Ammonites, as recorded in 1 Samuel chapter 11. Prior to this Saul had been proclaimed by Samuel as the king of Israel at Mizpah. Saul had gone home afterwards and gone about his business. Sometime later Nahash the Ammonite came up and besieged Jabesh-gilead. The men of Jabesh offered to make a covenant with the Ammonites in which they would serve them. Nahash responded that he would covenant with the men on the condition that the Ammonites gouge out the right eye of each of the men in order to shame all of Israel. The men of Jabesh were able to send out messengers to all of Israel asking for deliverance. When a messenger came to Gibeah, Saul's home territory, the people began to weep. Saul, coming in from plowing the fields, asked what the problem was. When he heard of the threat against the people of Jabesh the Spirit of God came on Saul mightily and he became very angry. He then sent out a message throughout all the territory of Israel, instructing the men to gather to him. With an army of 330,000 he then led a completely successful battle against their enemies and brought deliverance to the people of Jabesh.

This story is important in that it clearly indicates two things about Saul. One, he was anointed and called by the Holy Spirit. He was in no way a 'self-appointed, self-anointed leader'. Secondly, he did, at least on this occasion, respond and follow the leading of God. He was not a leader afraid to follow God into battle. He could be led by the Holy Spirit, one of the main characteristics of a *'son of God'*, according to Romans 8:15.

The ending of this particular story, however, gives even greater insight into the good that was in Saul's heart. When Saul had first been proclaimed by Samuel as king there had been men who had despised him and tried to reject him. Saul, however, had remained silent and not tried to either defend himself or take action against them. In this instance, he showed the same response as David would later when faced by threats against his status or position. After his powerful victory over the Ammonites, many of the people were then jealous for Saul and wanted to gather the men who had despised Saul as king and wanted to put them to death. But Saul responded:

> *'No one shall be put to death today, for this day the* Lord
> *has rescued Israel.'* (1 Samuel 11:13)

Instead of vengeful pettiness, Saul responded in mercy towards his critics. Even more importantly, he did not take the glory for the battle but gave it to God. Again it is important to understand Saul was a man who loved God and could serve Him.

It was not until Saul was firmly established as king over all Israel that the problems really began to surface. In 1 Samuel 13 we can read of Saul being controlled by a human, rather than prophetic view of what God could do against Israel's enemies the Philistines. In chapter 14 Saul responded religiously to the move of God through Jonathan against the Philistines. Saul made a religious oath rather than simply entering into what God was doing. That oath cost them a greater victory and almost cost him the life of Jonathan, his son. Chapter 15 records Saul's disobedience to the prophetic voice of God due to selfishness. These are the accounts of Saul's mistakes. But the question that needs to be asked, is how this could happen to a man that loved God?

Jesus stated that the good man spoke out of the treasure within his heart. One of the first signs we see of a lack of wholeness, or *teleios*, in Saul's heart is at Mizpah, when Samuel wanted to proclaim him as king. Saul was chosen by lot, from his family, which in turn was chosen from his tribe, in turn from all the tribes. When his name was called and he was sought after he was found hiding behind the baggage. Unfortunately, this is a picture of many of us. Inside of us, born by the Holy Spirit is a man or women of God. But all too often we are hiding behind our baggage of the past. Our past wounds and hurts, our past fears and failures tend to dominate our self-images. Proverbs 23, verse 7 reads:

'As he (a man) *thinks within himself, so he is.'*   (NAS)

The antidote for destructive self-image is to bring our hurts, sins and failures into God's light.

Beyond a shadow of a doubt Saul was called and anointed by God, But unlike David his successor, he was unwilling to be open and vulnerable before God. David, when exposed by Nathan the prophet for his sin with Bathsheba, cried out to God for forgiveness. Saul, when confronted by Samuel the prophet, lashed out grasping and tearing Samuel's garments. As Proverbs 27, verse 17 says:

> *'As iron sharpens iron, so one man sharpens another.'*

God allows conflict to come as a way of dealing with hurts and sin in our hearts. When we respond to God's compassion we find help, forgiveness, and healing. Proverbs 28, verse 13 says:

> *'He who conceals his sins does not prosper, but whoever confesses and renounces them finds mercy.'*

When we do not respond out of trust in the Father's mercy and grace, in our own strength we become defensive and grasping, moving then into denial, and from there into scapegoating. Denial and scapegoating are two classic signs of abusive churches.

What is of interest here is that Saul did trust in God's sovereignty as he was first coming into his kingship. Later however, when firmly established, he found it harder and harder to not be dominated by his personal baggage. The man of God became more and more obscured and the fleshly, or carnal man, became more visible. When Jesus withstood Satan's tempting in the wilderness before He began His ministry, Luke 4:13 says that Satan departed from Jesus *'until an opportune time'* came. When we looked at 'Henry' in chapter one, we saw how Satan specifically waited until he could do the most damage. Satan waited until there was a sizeable number of people under Henry that he could mess up. Hurts and insecurities that may just be a nagging thing at one point, can become major vulnerabilities when major responsibilities come.

When Jesus said that the prince of this world, or Satan, had nothing on Him it was at a very strategic time. He was nearing the time of His arrest, torture, and crucifixion. At His hour of greatest conflict, or stress, Jesus was free to do all that the Father wanted Him to do because there was no baggage He was carrying around. There were no hooks by which the enemy could manipulate Him. Paul warned us to avoid the sin which so easily entangles us. Sometimes those sins are of the heart, such as jealousy and bitterness, and usually those hooks stem from a deep-rooted insecurity and fear of rejection. This is why Proverbs 4:23 reads:

> *'Above all else, guard your heart, for it is the wellspring of life.'*

The battle is as much within as without. The Holy Spirit within us is calling out *'Abba, Father'*. The old carnal man within us is trying to grasp, control, and manipulate.

In a sense we could say Saul represents the old carnal man on the throne while David is like the new man in Christ. Both were imperfect, but David lived in God's grace while Saul lived by his own strength, much of the time. From the beginning David's story was not completely different from Saul's. When Saul was prophesied over by Samuel, he was looking for his father's lost donkeys. When Samuel came to the house of Jesse, David, his son, was out in the fields looking after the sheep. They were both young men taken from relative obscurity and promoted into the national spotlight. At first we see real similarities. Saul chose to forgive the men who had despised him when he came into power. David in turn, chose not to run way or to attack Saul when Saul began to grow jealous of him. The differences began to be visible when authority and heavy responsibility, together with the ensuing stress, came.

God gave directions to Saul, via Samuel, in 1 Samuel 13, to wait seven days for Samuel's arrival, then God would give them victory over the Philistines even though they were vastly outnumbered by them. Saul however, due to the overwhelming odds against him and his men, began to grow nervous and fearful. His unbelief led him into sin. Rather than obeying the directions of the Lord, he initiated the peace offering himself before Samuel's arrival. When Samuel arrived he rebuked Saul and prophesied that his kingdom would not endure (1 Samuel 13:5–14). On the face of it, this appears as just a simple matter of faith; who is bigger – God or the huge Philistine army? It certainly is a matter of faith, but not just faith in the principles of God, but faith in a relationship with God. Jesus stated that one must be both converted **and** become as a child to experience the Kingdom of God. Jesus Himself, only did the things He **saw** the Father doing. His Spirit, the Holy Spirit, within us is constantly attempting to promote a child-like cry for intimacy with the Father. Here, in essence, was Saul's shortcoming. Being a true reflection, or king, of Israel at that time he knew how to perform the religious offering. He knew how to fight in his own strength. What he did not know was how to walk in a child-like trust of God's goodness and provision. God's perfect, *teleios*, love casts out fear. We all from time to time, experience fear gnawing at our soul. Sometimes, we can summon the wherewithal from ourselves to press on, despite the opposition or obstacle. But often, God allows completely overwhelming situations to fall in our laps. Not because He is against us, but because He desires us to learn to trust Him and lean into His goodness, strength, and provision. This was Saul's downfall. He did love God to a degree, and he understood the principles and precepts of God to a degree. His problem was that unlike David, he did not have a heart-to-heart relationship, or personal friendship with God.

One of the things that Saul and David had in common is that at times they both flagrantly disobeyed God. With David we can think of his adultery with Bathsheba and then the murder of her husband Uriah in an attempt to cover up her pregnancy. What is critical in understanding our study of leaders and their relationship to God, is not whether David and Saul were perfect, but whether they trusted in God's love and goodness. When David was exposed by the prophet Nathan for his sins with Bathsheba and the murder of Uriah he responded by seeking God. Psalm 51 contains

David's cry of repentance to the Lord. The first three verses
read:

> *'Have mercy on me, O God, according to your unfailing love;*
> *according to your great compassion blot out my transgres-*
> *sions. Wash away all my iniquity and cleanse me from my*
> *sin. For I know my transgressions, and my sin is always*
> *before me. Against you, you only, have I sinned and done*
> *what is evil in your sight, so that you are proved right when*
> *you speak and justified when you judge.'*

David, in his heart, realized God was a God of compassion
and love, slow to anger and abounding in loving kindness and truth. Saul, on the other hand, due to lack of
intimacy with God, was ignorant of His heart. Saul ended up
committing a sin which is common to all of us at times. Saul
was confronted by Samuel for his disobedience in not
destroying all of the enemy and booty after the battle
against the Amalekites in 1 Samuel 15. The prophetic
directions God had given him were to destroy everyone
and everything captured. Saul, out of greed, kept the best of
the sheep, and the livestock, and everything good. He only
destroyed what was worthless. When Samuel arrived after
the battle Saul went into a mode of denial. He proclaimed
that they had fully carried out the directions of the Lord.
Samuel's classic response was:

> *'What then is this bleating of sheep in my ears? What is this*
> *lowing of cattle that I hear?'*

Saul again answered in denial of his sin. He said that they
had saved the best to make a sacrifice to the Lord.

Denial is one of the classic symptoms of abusive leaders.
When questioned, even in a humble and gentle manner by
members of the church, they will often give a 'religious'
answer in order to cover up their hurts and/or sins. David, as
we have already seen, was a sinner the same as Saul. Paul the
apostle who turned his world upside down with the gospel,

freely admitted that he fell short of God's standards. Paul wrote to the church in Rome:

'For what I want to do I do not do, but what I hate I do.'
(Romans 7:15)

But Paul, like David, realized his hope was in God's mercy and grace, not in his self-righteousness. Therefore, they were free to admit their sins rather than going into a mode of denial. Like the story of Pinocchio, the wooden boy whose nose grew every time he lied, a denial mode has a way of becoming more and more pronounced. For leaders caught up in a denial mode there is always a reason for the problems. There is constant justification, be it spiritual warfare, unbelief, or a Jezebel in the camp that has brought on the problems. The hard part for those caught up with an abused church is that often those problems **are** a reality. Unbelief **can** prevent a church from moving into greater fruitfulness. There are often Jezebels in a church who are on a mission to undermine church leadership. The issue for some, however, is that these types of problems become a cover-up. If denial goes on indefinitely, whether with an individual or a group, it goes into a deeper and more dangerous stage of scapegoating, which will be discussed later in the book.

As judgement came on Saul from God, God's Spirit and anointing lifted off him. In desperation, Saul arranged for David the shepherd boy to come and minister to him with his harp and song (1 Samuel 16:14–23). Saul loved David greatly. He recognized the gifting and grace on his life and took David to be his armor bearer. Later on when David slew Goliath, Saul appointed him as one of his army commanders. And this is where the problems between Saul and David really began.

When David and his men would parade into the city after his victories, the people would sing *'there is Saul who has slain thousands, and there is David who has slain his tens of thousands.'* Saul grew increasingly jealous of David to the point where he tried to kill him by his own hand as well as by skullduggery. Saul's surface problem was jealousy, but the root issue was a hurting heart. Rather than being rooted and grounded in God's love for him, his popularity, stature, and empire were essential to his ego. The fact is, even though Saul was king over the land he was a slave to his own insecurity.

Many years later David was faced with a reverse problem. He now was king, with a popular son who was attempting to overthrow him. His response however was the exact opposite of Saul's. David's son Absalom brought a rebellion against David's kingship. The rebels were successful to the point that David had to flee Jerusalem to save the city from being destroyed. Later, however, David and his followers came to the place where they were prepared to go to battle against the other tribes which were following his son. David gave the order that if it was at all possible, his son was not to be harmed for David's sake.

David, unlike Saul, did not see his prestige and power as things to be fought for at all costs. He wrote in Psalm 73 verse 26:

'My flesh and my heart may fail, but God is the strength of my heart and my portion forever.'

His strength did not stem from man, but rather from God's love and faithfulness. As a young man living the lonely life of a shepherd he learned of God's care and provision. In the famous shepherd's psalm, David wrote:

'The LORD is my shepherd, I shall not be in want. He makes me lie down in green pastures, he leads me beside quiet waters, he restores my soul. He guides me in paths of righteousness for his name's sake. Even though I walk through the valley of the shadow of death, I will fear no evil, for you are with me; your rod and your staff, they comfort me. You prepare a table before me in the presence of my enemies. You anoint my head with oil; my cup

overflows. Surely goodness and love will follow me all the days of my life, and I will dwell in the house of the LORD forever.' (Psalm 23)

David's sense of security and significance was derived from God's love. 1 John 4:18 states that God's perfect love casts out fear. Jesus stated in Luke 18 that, *'whoever does not receive the kingdom of God like a child shall not enter it at all.'* There are several things necessary to qualify as a good leader. Gifting, calling, leadership skills, and experience are all part of the requirements. But because ministry that bears true fruit comes from the heart, a child-like relationship with the Father is perhaps the greatest requirement. David's unquenchable love of God was what qualified him to be God's man. Saul's distrust of God's love and provision was what disqualified him from continuing to lead God's people. Saul was king over Israel, but God was not King over Saul. It's impossible for a leader of God's people to truly lead the sheep into the green pastures unless he, or she, are themselves truly sheep of God's pasture.

Chapter 7

Jezebels, Rebels and Witches

It seems that when the inevitable fallout begins in churches suffering spiritual abuse, accusation and labels begin to fly. Usually those labels and accusations are centered around one if not all three of the following; Jezebels, witchcraft, and rebellion. I would like to take a brief look at the biblical definition of what these three terms really mean. It would probably take a whole book to do justice to these three topics and the problems they cause in church and society. For our purposes, however, we will look at these problems briefly in order to better understand abuse from leaders to church members and vice versa.

Jezebels

The first mention of Jezebel in the Bible is 1 Kings 16, verse 31. According to verse 30 King Ahab did more evil than all the kings before him. His chief sin, perhaps, that brought about the most damage for the Northern kingdom was to marry Jezebel. Jezebel was a princess of the city and area of Sidon. Sidon was located in Phoenicia, today the nation of Syria. The Sidonians practised several things that were (and are) major sin. The root problem was that they did not worship Jehovah, but rather Baal. Baal means lord and possessor. A god which demanded a master/slave relationship with his people. Some scholars believe there is a tie-in with the false god Bel of Babylon as well as Zeus of Greece. Ashtoreth, the 'queen of heaven' was also worshipped by the Phoenicans as the wife of Baal.

The sin of Ahab was in not only marrying a woman from outside of Israel but that he also imported her faith and demonic practices. There were three major sins Jezebel would have imported from Sidon. Firstly, denying the Lord God Jehovah, secondly, bringing temple prostitution into the worship (a practice of some of the Phoenicians), and thirdly, bringing in false prophets and priests of Baal. Jezebel also had a love of operating in the spiritual realm outside of the Kingdom of God. What today is called e.s.p., tele-kinetics, spiritualistic healings, etc., was common practice with the prophets and priests of Baal. We could generalize the three major traits of a Jezebel as firstly; rebellion against God and His authority while at the same time having a love of the spiritual realm. Secondly, a focus on sexual immoral-ity, and thirdly a desire for spiritual gifts and powers outside the Kingdom of God, and moving in those demonic giftings for selfish purposes.

Satan is unable to really create since he himself is only a created being. His general practice is twofold. Either he tries with evil intent to imitate what God does, or he tries to pollute what God has created and/or established. Just as there is a holy trinity of God the Father, God the Son, and God the Holy Spirit there is also a false and evil trinity. That cheap counterfeit being Satan the father of lies, the anti-christ, and the Jezebel spirit or spirit of witchcraft. The spirit of Jezebel, being the evil counterfeit to the Holy Spirit, is characterized by spiritual power, gifting, and authority, with the difference being that the source is demonic. Unfortun-ately this difference is not always obvious when that warfare comes against a church.

Before we talk about the typical working of a true Jezebel in a church setting today, it is important to point out some things to give parameters to our thinking. There seems to be a predisposition among many churches and leaders to do two things with the label Jezebel. First, to assume that when any conflict arises with a woman involved in ministry, or desiring to be involved in ministry, that she is 'a Jezebel' or under the influence of a Jezebel spirit. Secondly, to assume that the Jezebel spirit or problem is something that can only happen to women. The basis for this is the fact that in the two biblical situations in the Bible with 'a Jezebel', 1 and 2 Kings, and Revelation 2, verse 20, both are described as a woman. There is no firm basis for stating that only women can be vulnerable to the Jezebel spirit. One of the primary ways in which a Jezebel makes inroads into a church is through seduction – whether emotionally, spiritually, or sexually. It is all too common to equate seduction with women only. The fact is, however, that any individual, male or female, is susceptible when they have a heart motivated by greed, envy, or jealousy. Just because the Bible only names two female Jezebels, we can by no means rule out males being under a Jezebel influence.

The argument that since women are the weaker vessel they are more susceptible to be used by a Jezebel, also holds little water. It is my belief that, in general, women should not be senior pastors or leaders of churches, but I have seen exceptions to that. The biblical admonishment in 1 Corinthians 14 that women should not speak in church is not concerned with women in leadership, but rather **women (and men) not causing a disturbance by asking questions during services.** The call is to do all things decently and in order. The Bible speaks of women such as the four daughters of Philip **who were prophetesses**, and seem to have been in some form of leadership. Even in Old Testament times God used women such as Deborah, a prophetess and a judge, who along with Barak led the Israelite people into victory against their enemies. It is true women are the weaker vessels in some ways, but in Christ Jesus there is neither male or female, slave or free; we are all one in Christ Jesus. Unfortunately, many Christian men have over-emphasized some scriptures to justify their view of women as second-class citizens in the church.

What is also important to remember here, is that in the account of Jezebel in 1 Kings, it was a male in leadership who allowed her to come into position and authority. There is hardly ever a Jezebel situation, where a leader, usually a male and one lacking in discernment or strength, did not first give that Jezebel a position. So, let's look at the beginning of the syndrome – the Ahab, or Jezebel facilitator, who is weak enough to be seduced by the seduction.

At this point, it would be helpful to point out that there is a 'spirit of seduction'. Satan's downfall, according to Isaiah 14:14 was pride. He desired to be *'like the Most High.'* This was the same temptation he caught Adam and Eve with. He came as a snake and seduced them with the lie that if they ate of the tree of knowledge they could be *'as God.'* Seduction, the arts, and the more mystical side of ministry seem to often go hand in hand. Ezekiel, speaking of Satan, metaphorically identifying the King of Tyre, said:

> *'You were the model of perfection, full of wisdom and perfect in beauty. You were in Eden, the garden of God; every precious stone adorned you: ruby, topaz and emerald, chrysolite, onyx and jasper, sapphire, turquoise and beryl. Your settings and mountings were made of gold; on the day you were created they were prepared. You were anointed as a guardian cherub, for so I ordained you. You were on the holy mount of God; you walked among the fiery stones. You were blameless in your ways from the day you were created till wickedness was found in you.'* (Ezekiel 28:12–15)

Isaiah referred to Satan's 'harps'. Satan as chief of the angels, the *'anointed cherub who covers'* probably had the function of being the chief worship leader. Being the most beautiful of all God's created beings he was to have been a reflection of the beauty of God. His sin was getting caught up in his own beauty and wanting to take the glory for himself. Satan, being then thrown out of God's eternal presence, turned his beauty towards the art of seduction.

The arts are a wonderful gift of God to mankind. We think of many of the greatest artist of the renaissance, who, as artists, were primarily concerned with employing their God-given talents to glorify God. When talent, gifts, skills, or beauty is used by artists to primarily focus on themselves or mankind they enter into Satan's downfall. Because Satan was an artist himself and beautiful, he loves to use both beauty and the arts to seduce people away from God.

Women in general are more captivated by verbal communication. Men, on the other hand, are more easily beguiled visually. Satan first seduced Eve, and then Eve in turn seduced Adam into disobedience towards God's commandments. But this also gives us insight into the working of a Jezebel spirit. Queen Jezebel probably imported not only a demonic, overt, focus on sensuality, but temple prostitution as well.[1] Temple prostitution was common with most of Israel's neighbours. In Revelation chapter 2, verse 20, Jesus rebuked the church of Thyatira for tolerating 'that woman Jezebel' who called herself a prophetess and led some of Jesus' servants into sexual immorality. Not exclusively so, but often when a woman is under the influence of a Jezebel spirit she will use her femininity to seduce leadership under her influence. A man under the influence of a Jezebel spirit will use flattering words and a false sense of compassion and empathy to woo people away from God's ordained leadership of a church.

Because the prophetic and artistic processes of creativity are so similar, there tends to be a high degree of prophetic and/or artistic people that are given over to a jezebelic influence. Again, the Jezebel of the book of Kings as well as Revelation 2, was involved in the prophetic, worship, and inciting immorality. I doubt if there are any statistics on this, but in being involved in the international church scene for 15 years it is frightening how many churches I have seen devastated by immorality. And usually that immorality takes place between people that are involved in the ministry at a high level. Many pastor's or elder's wives have been seduced by worship leaders. Likewise many pastors have been seduced by hard working women in the church who appear to love God and flow somewhat in the prophetic.

It is important to understand, however, that the true purpose of a Jezebel is to deliberately undermine the authority of God-given leadership and lead people into the occult and immorality. It is equally important to realize what a Jezebel is not. Someone who merely asks questions of the leadership from a standpoint of humility, is not a Jezebel. Someone who is burnt out and needs a season away from responsibility in the church is not a Jezebel. Someone who has a theological difference, or a philosophical dispute with leadership and believes that God wants them elsewhere, is not necessarily either a rebel or a Jezebel. A person operating under a Jezebel influence either knowingly or not, is on a mission to usurp authority away from leadership for **their own gain.**

The unfortunate truth is that there are many Jezebels at work in many churches. An unfortunate side effect of that has been that many leaders who are afraid of searching out the truth, resort to accusations of Jezebel when in fact, there may be another reason altogether for their problems.

Rebellion

Rebellion and witchcraft, brother and sister, are the offspring of the Jezebel spirit. In 1 Samuel chapter 15, verse 23, the prophet Samuel told King Saul:

> '... *rebellion is like the sin of divination* (witchcraft), *and arrogance like the evil of idolatry.*'

The word of the Lord to Saul had been to utterly destroy all of the people, livestock, and booty of the Amalekites. Instead, Saul destroyed that which was worthless, but kept the best for himself and his followers. When Samuel rebuked Saul, Saul responded with a religious justification that he had kept them in order to make a sacrifice. This is an important point, which we will refer to later.

Webster's *New Collegiate Dictionary* defines rebelling as 'opposition to one in authority or dominance'. Webster's is of course concerned with understanding from man's perspective. Biblically, rebellion is disobedience to God. Mankind left the Garden of intimacy with God and entered into the domain of rebellion, or disobedience, when Adam and Eve ate of the forbidden fruit. Every time sin is committed, we have made a choice to do what we desire to do. When King Saul did not fully obey God, he made a decision to do what he wanted to do contrary to the will of God. There is no one perfect. Isaiah the prophet said that the best we can come up with is as a dirty rag to God's holiness. But the difference between Saul and David's sins was vast. David visited the domain of rebellion, whereas Saul's heart was captivated by it. The New Testament makes a clear difference between those who fall into sin as opposed to those who practice sin as a lifestyle.

The fact is that Saul's heart was motivated by greed. He disobeyed God because of idolatry in his life. He **idolized** riches and power. It went against his heart to destroy the best of the livestock and wealth he had captured from the Amalekites. His root problem as we have already discussed was a heart not centered on God. Because he lacked God's perfect love his tendency was to trust in position and riches, which was very different from David.

But there is also a deeper level of rebellion that is very much in evidence in today's cultures: that is rebellion stemming from pride of life. Pride was Satan's downfall. This was the temptation he offered Adam and Eve. Pride is the inward desire to promote one's self. God's call on each of us is to deny one's self and to actually die to one's self. This is the divine route to fulfillment.

So many struggles in life are due to pride. Job disputes, divorces, political strife, and warfare usually boil down to pride – a person or group, wanting to exert themself over another. The prophet Samuel equated Saul's disobedience with **arrogance**. Arrogance is to boldly assert your will against others. It is often coupled with rebellion. Due to the breakdown of the family unit over the last several generations we now have a massive problem in the western world with individuals ruled by pride of self. This can be seen on a larger scale by the increasing fragmentation taking place in society. Over thirty years ago, Martin Luther King gave a brilliant speech calling out for a 'color blind' society. A society in which his black children could grow and live in a culture that took no notice of their skin color. Today although the same language is used there is an increasing move towards fragmentation among most ethnic groups, including Caucasian.

These tendencies are also visible in many churches. We have many 'saved' people who are involved in churches and ministry but are often motivated by arrogance and idolatry of self. This can be seen in many Christians who have the habit of 'church hopping'. These are Christians who rarely stay at a church for more than a year or so. They are always looking for the 'perfect church'. They will stay at a church until they begin to find flaws in the church or leadership. At that point they become disillusioned and move on. In reality, most of them are people who do not want to deal with issues and sin in their lives. They will love a church during the honeymoon stage. But as soon as the preaching gets a little too convicting, the pastor is getting away from really preaching the gospel. They will go to a home group until the other members start meddling and finding fault with them. In reality the Holy Spirit is trying to use different members of the body to bring healing and wholeness, but rebellion too often rules the heart.

People who end up in classic spiritually abusive churches rarely fall into this category. In fact, they can often be faulted for being overly loyal in a fanatical sense. They tend to be loyal to the point of ignoring blatant misuse of scripture and people. They represent the opposite side of the pendulum. Like all pendulums, however, when it swings it first goes all the way towards the other extreme.

Many legitimate victims of spiritual abuse after leaving a toxic church, are then so gun-shy that they feel any pastoral authority at all is deeply threatening. It is at that point that if they do not open up to healing, forgiveness, and possible counseling, they could end up severely alienated from the rest of the body. If left unattended their wounds can get so completely infected through pride and anger that they will end up cancerous with bitterness.

Often, as with the label of Jezebel, the term 'rebellious' is misused. A healthy pastor will look beyond the annoyance of bleating sheep to find out why they are troubled. An immature or uncaring pastor will merely take offence at the sheep who does not enthusiastically fall into place. And as with the case of false Jezebel accusations, there is a place for questions to be asked in humility.

An individual who is a committed member of a church should be able to approach the church leadership and ask questions. That statement implies two things; firstly, that a church member is someone who is involved in relationships in the church, is tithing, and who is contributing time and energy as part of the church family. Secondly, that they come in humility to leaders. I do not mean sackcloth and ashes, but an attitude of respect for God's delegated leaders. And thirdly, that they are asking not demanding.

Recently, while taking a break from a conference session in England I was seated with three friends in the conference center cafeteria. Two of these friends were also speakers at the conference. A middle-aged woman got up from a nearby table and approached us. She informed us that her twenty-something daughter, at the table with her, had been severely depressed for years after being in a Satanist group. She then said that God had just told her that if one of us would minister to her daughter, she would be set free. All of us realized that any attempt at ministry would take several hours and would only open her up. It would have not been a favor to the daughter to have only offered her a partial healing. She then proceeded to rebuke us and let us know that because of leaders 'like us' she had once left Christianity.

What she was completely unaware of was that she was in a very arrogant place of demanding. Love, gifts, and service in Christ's Name should always be understood in the framework of love, not demands. After more abuse the women walked back to her table. All of us understood that we had just seen a classic bit of Jezebel manipulation. Although this woman probably was saved, she has probably been an extreme pain in several pastor's lives.

One of the reasons there are so many church splits among charismatic-type churches today is pride. Everyone claims that they have heard from God and if the leadership does not fall into line with 'their word' they are in sin. By very definition a leader needs to lead or else he is not really a leader. Critics often denounce the pastor and say he needs first and last to be a 'servant of the people' because that was what Jesus was. That is only half of the picture of Jesus, however. He was constantly serving the people and the disciples. In fact, Jesus stated Himself, that He came to serve rather than being served. But on the other hand He always led the disciples, and not vice versa. When Peter tried to tell Jesus not to go to Jerusalem and be arrested, Jesus rebuked the demonic influence affecting Peter. There are no scriptural examples of Jesus ever being anything less than a leader. A serving leader yes, but still a leader who led His disciples.

One of the interesting things about Saul's response to Samuel's rebuke was he attempted to religiously justify himself. He stated that he had merely kept the best of the livestock in order to make a sacrifice to the Lord. Samuel's famous response was that God preferred obedience to sacrifice. This passage gives a helpful key in being able to determine spiritual rebellion. When Satan attempted to tempt Jesus in the wilderness he quoted scripture as part of his bag of tricks. Paul, in speaking of deception, said that even *'Satan himself masquerades as an angel of light.'* The religious spirit stemming from the antichrist, is one of the most powerfully deceptive of all demonic deceptions because it hides behind religious facades and words. Often someone fomenting rebellion within a church or ministry will attempt to justify their actions or words with religious jargon and even scripture taken out of context. Saul's excuse was that he wanted to *'make a sacrifice for the Lord.'*

Often, insecure leaders will fall prey to 'scapegoating'. They will use scriptural accusations, using terms like 'rebel' or 'Jezebel', to attack people that they have a personal problem with. On the other hand countless Christians who are filled with bitterness and anger will spiritualize their real rebellion against leaders with religious justification. Again to contrast David and Saul, we see a marked difference in how they responded to sin in their lives. Saul went into religious justification on at least two occasions when he disobeyed the Lord.[2] David, on the other hand, when confronted by his deep sin of adultery and murder (2 Samuel 12:13) cried out to the Lord in repentance and said:

> *'Hide your face from my sins and blot out all my iniquity. Create in me a pure heart, O God, and renew a steadfast spirit within me. Do not cast me from your presence or take your Holy Spirit from me. Restore to me the joy of your salvation and grant me a willing spirit, to sustain me ... You do not delight in sacrifice, or I would bring it; you do not take pleasure in burnt offerings. The sacrifices of God are a broken spirit; a broken and contrite heart, O God, you will not despise.'* (Psalm 51:9–17)

Because pride is the root issue with rebellion, an individual in rebellion, when confronted, will usually resort to a religious justification. Scripture will be quoted and spiritual-sounding excuses will be offered. The individual who is gossiping about someone else always knows gossip is a sin. They will say however, that they are not gossiping but trying to 'alert' other brothers and sisters to pray for the sorrowful victim of their concern. The brother who has caused two other church splits will admit the pastor is called to lead, but for the 'sake of the church' they have to stand up for the truth.

The issue of rebellion in churches is very much a two-sided one. There are unfortunately pastors who use that label routinely as a defence mechanism in an incorrect way. However, there is a major problem in the church today with rebellion, especially as the last two generations are made up of individuals who often want to 'do their own thing', no matter what the consequences. It is an age-old problem going all the way back to the original sin. Not the sin of Adam and Eve, but of Satan in heaven being self-centered rather than God-centered. As Hebrews 13:17 reads:

> *'Obey your leaders and submit to their authority. They keep watch over you as men who must give an account. Obey them so that their work will be a joy, not a burden, for that would be of no advantage to you.'*

There is a time for leaving a toxic church, which we will discuss later. That situation though is really not the case for many who are standing in arrogance and rebellion.

Witchcraft

For a basic insight into witchcraft, we will, as with rebellion, look at Samuel's response to Saul's disobedience in 1 Samuel. Samuel said to Saul that his rebellion (disobedience) was as the sin of divination (witchcraft). The biblical definition of rebellion is very simply disobedience towards God's authority. In the Garden of Eden Adam and Eve disobeyed God by eating of the forbidden fruit. Jesus stated in John 14:15:

> *'If you love Me, you will obey what I command.'*

Obedience is always a measure of love towards the Lord and leadership.

Saul's disobedience went into a deeper dimension of rebellion, however. His disobedience was not just out of disrespect, but for his own gain. Samuel added to his

rebuke of King Saul that *'arrogance was as the evil of idolatry.'*
Witchcraft and idolatry go hand in hand. Idolatry means the
worship of something or someone other than the Lord.
Exodus 20:3–4 reads:

> *'You shall have no other gods before me. You shall not make
> for yourself an idol in the form of anything in heaven above
> or on the earth beneath or in the waters below.'*

James wrote that *'the spirit he caused to live in us envies
intensely.'* God hates idolatry because it robs us of being able
to focus on Him and His great love for us. Witchcraft in
essence is operating in the spiritual realm for the purpose of
serving either self or someone else.

In the case of Saul's disobedience it was a more serious
offence than normal straightforward insubordination. First
of all, he was using his God-given authority to bring about
his own increase. That was witchcraft. Secondly, he preferred
the treasure of the silver and gold and the sheep and the
oxen over the will of God. His arrogance in defying God's
complete will stemmed from the idolatry of riches. When a
spiritual leader, or individual, uses their position, talents,
and God-given authority for their own gain – that is witchcraft!

It is the case of many Christians that they are saved and
going to heaven, but somehow they have wandered from
their first love. The value system of the world can begin to
permeate their motives. They may still be preaching the
gospel, teaching the word, and healing the sick, but somehow their heart motivation is to build their empire instead
of God's Kingdom.

In pentecostal and charismatic-type churches there seems
to be more 'Christian witchcraft' going on, compared to
other evangelical churches. We know from the story of
Balaam that even a donkey can prophesy when there is an
anointing from God. Romans 11:29 says that *'the gifts and
calling of God are without repentance.'* Often God will anoint
an individual, such as Saul, whom God knows in His

omniscience will fall away from his or her first love. Partially, this is due to the fact that God loves to heal and save the lost and the broken and is not nearly as particular as we are concerning the messenger. Partially it is because God in His omniscience sees the end of all things which is hidden from us. But for whatever reason, there is a phenomena of Christians using spiritual gifts primarily for their own gain.

This high degree of giftedness is one of the greatest hooks Satan uses in keeping people in bondage to an abusive church, and presents two real problems for the church, or any Christians involved. First, unless there is some oversight with true spiritual discernment, left unchecked it will wreak complete havoc. Giftedness may be evidenced in the preaching and teaching, or in evangelism, or a powerful prophetic or healing anointing. Almost always the language used is 'theologically correct'. The words and teaching are usually very biblical sounding. But it is the heart, the motivation, that is off. This is the chief reason why many Christians in an abusive church wait such a long time to leave. They know they are being used and manipulated. They know they are becoming more and more uneasy with teaching that is theologically off, but how can their negative thoughts about that leader be correct when there is such a wonderful anointing?

Secondly, there will be an impartation of 'ambition' to the followers of that leader. That is to say, the disciple will be far more focused on the money, numbers and outward signs of success than they will be on the person of God. There we find the principle I call 'spiritual dynamics'. Spiritual dynamics means, basically, that the disciples of a leader become the reflection of who their leaders are, not merely what they say. Jesus warned the people to do all that the Pharisees said, but not what they did, because of their hypocrisy. When an individual joins a church family, they will be a recipient of the spiritual flow down through the leadership. If the leadership is healthy the disciples will grow more and more healthy. Likewise, if the leadership is spiritually or emotionally unhealthy, that too will be imparted to the followers. If there is a demonic stronghold on the leadership such as idolatry of riches, or love of prestige that too will become part of the package of their followers.

Can one be a born again Christian and involved in witchcraft? Emphatically, yes. Perhaps not the overt witchcraft of witches in the popular sense, but witchcraft in using spiritual gifts and authority for personal gain rather than for God and the hurt and lost. To help put things into perspective, however, it should be noted that there are many, many leaders having to deal with Christian witchcraft in church members who are after position and authority. It is not only leadership which can be seduced by a jezebelic influence. Basically, any individual whose heart is not centered on living for God is vulnerable to seeking their kingdom rather than purely God's.

Notes

1. *Harper's Bible Dictionary*, Miller 1952, p. 587.
2. 1 Samuel 13:8–14 and 1 Samuel 15:15.

Chapter 8

Why Legalism is Sin!

'If the Spirit of Grace is absent, the Law is present only to convict and kill.'   (Agaustine of Hippo)

'The law was added so that the trespass might increase. But where sin increased, grace increased all the more.'
(The Apostle Paul, Romans 5:20)

To address the issue of grace versus legalism in one chapter is to do a severe injustice to the topic. To understand the damage done to multitudes by primarily focusing on the law as opposed to God's grace would take at least one whole book of serious depth. What we will try to cover over the next few pages is a limited discussion of how legalism in an abusive church is as gasoline to a fire.

By very nature, toxic faith type churches lean towards legalism. The legalism may take on various shades and hues. In some churches, despite preaching a gospel of grace, the outward do's and don'ts, or the performance, take precedence over what Jesus accomplished on the cross. For the sake of staying focused on the theme of spiritual abuse we will be looking at two of the most common forms of legalism that tend to run rampant in many abusive churches.

The first and most obvious type of spiritual abuse through legalism is what we could call 'the cross plus' syndrome. In essence, the cross plus syndrome is where people know they are brought into relationship with God by grace, i.e. the cross. Thereafter however, the ongoing relationship with the Lord and one another is determined by their performance. In short, if the believer arrives at a high standard of outward holiness they are led to believe that God really loves them. Usually that standard is determined by the particular Christian culture of that denomination or the leader's background.

Usually, leaders who abuse followers by focusing on legalism see no 'grey areas' at all. A grey area would be something that is not spelled out completely as righteous or sinful in the Bible. Areas such as whether Christians ought to drink wine, or use birth control, or watch movies, or listen to secular music, etc. As an example, let us look at one of the common stands made in legalistic churches in a grey area.

The argument has been made by some that while wine was drunk in the early church, it was non-alcoholic. Wine, in fact, was alcoholic during the times of Noah, David, and Solomon. When we read in the Psalms or Proverbs about drinking wine there is usually a warning about excess, which clearly means the wine was alcoholic. Before the time of refrigeration fruit drinks as we think of them today were just not an option. The criticism of the 120 in the upper room that they were drunk on the day of Pentecost, makes no sense if the wine was non-alcoholic (Acts 2:13). Most leaders who say it is sin for a Christian to drink any alcoholic beverage have never tried to figure Deuteronomy 14:26 into their theology. Moses encouraged the people that if the designated city to give their tithe to was too far away, they were to use their tithe money on whatever they desired, including wine or any other fermented drink, and *'then you and your household shall eat there in the presence of the LORD your God and rejoice.'* Few would suggest that Moses was encouraging anyone to enter into sin.

Can drinking wine or alcohol be a sin? Clearly and emphatically, yes, in many situations it can be. Drinking to the point of intoxication is biblically wrong. Paul encouraged those who are free in certain areas not to exercise their freedom in front of those with a weaker faith (Romans 14:20–21). But in writing to Timothy (1 Timothy 5:23), Paul encouraged him to drink a little wine for the sake of his stomach. As in many 'grey areas' drinking alcohol needs to be decided by the individual on the basis of how the Spirit is leading him, who they are with, and their own personal history. Someone with a past problem of serious alcohol abuse should probably be encouraged not to partake at all, since the flashbacks to the old bondage could trigger things off. Any time a practical maxim is used exclusively at the expense of the Holy Spirit's leading, religious bondage is beginning to creep in. As Paul said, *'all those who are led by the Spirit are the sons of God.'*

This type of legalism is destructive over a long period in three basic ways. One, in essence this is the spirit, or power of man-made religion attempting to usurp our priesthood. Jesus died so that we might have intimacy restored with the Father. God desires intimacy so much that He places His own Spirit or presence within us when we are born again. This type of religious control is a subtle demonic attempt to rob us of being led by the Spirit and of responding to life's choices not just out of discipline, but out of the joy of responding to the Holy Spirit. Paul in Colossians 2:20–23, said the following concerning this issue:

> *'Since you died with Christ to the basic principles of this world, why, as though you still belonged to it, do you submit to its rules: "Do not handle! Do not taste! Do not touch!"? These are all destined to perish with use, because they are based on human commands and teachings. Such regulations indeed have an appearance of wisdom, with their self-imposed worship, their false humility and their harsh treatment of the body, but they lack any value in restraining sensual indulgence.'*

Secondly, over a period of time legalism manages to discourage the victim from seeking God's face and worshiping Him. One ends up focusing on oneself. As the prophet

Isaiah said so powerfully, *'all our righteous acts are like filthy rags'* (Isaiah 64:6). Paul stated that he did not want to be found with a righteousness derived from the law but rather in the grace of Jesus. Without a shadow of a doubt Christians are called to live lives of service, sacrifice, and righteousness. But, as we have already discussed, that lifestyle must come out of the joy of being obedient to the Lord in response to His Spirit, rather than out of feeble attempts to try to earn God's love. Again, as we previously discussed, God has not given us the spirit of slavery taking us into fear again, but rather the Spirit of adoption. As Paul said, the Spirit within us is crying out 'Abba, Father.'

This is the freedom of the cross – the freedom to know God and to be known by Him! When our primary emphasis is on earning things from God, we tend to be reluctant in worshiping God and seeking Him. After all, why should we dare to think we can approach Him, when we know what terrible sinners we are. In fact, many of us as Christians are filled with pride and other issues that can put up barriers between us and the Lord. But any time we fall back into the system of the law and trying to live perfectly in order to deserve God's love we are doomed. Paul called the Christians in the early church of Galatia 'foolish' because they had been seduced by this very deception.

God spoke through the prophet Hosea and said that no longer should the Israelites relate to the Lord God Jehovah, as Baali. Baali is a name of the false god Baal, which means master, as in a slave/master relationship. Rather they will know God as Ishi, meaning lover or husband, one who cares deeply for us. Over a period of time, Christians saved by grace but living in the cross plus legalism, can be robbed of even having basic faith in the nature of God and His inherent goodness and compassion.

Jesus said that when our adversary is taking us to court, we should agree with him quickly while on the way to court. If we dare to stand before God's throne in a posture of defence we will be found guilty every time. We must not forget we **are** sinners saved by grace. But when we agree with the accuser, trust in God's compassion and grace and confess our sins, God is quick to forgive and bring healing. Over a period of time people caught up in legalism cannot distinguish between the convicting voice of the Holy Spirit and the condemnation of Satan who wants to destroy us. When God chastises us, it is out of the motivation of love and healing. Satan longs to get his hooks of religion into our souls so that he can keep us always striving but always coming up short of perfection. One can subtly go from the loving regard of a loving God, to an unbiblical fear to reach out to Him. Over that period of time, Jesus is replaced by Baali – the false God of slavery. The good news slowly turns out to be the bad news.

The second area of legalism that many toxic churches fall into is the over-emphasis on the 'mission' to the neglect of relationship. By relationship I do not mean that the church members do not spend time together, although that too is often the case. What I am referring to is our evaluation of one another. Instead of seeing one another as unique gifts from God, created in His image and alive in His Spirit, we place a utilitarian value on one another; we no longer value each other for who we are. We value one another through what we can perform or contribute.

In the first sort of legalistic-type church we discussed, the root problem is usually a poor theology of grace. In the second type of church good theology can be in existence, but it is ignored, or run over by the 'ministry machine'. In this type of church if you are hurting or broken to the point that you are unable to contribute time, energy and money you are considered a second-class saint.

A good church, it has been said, is made up of four basic components; a training component, a fellowship component, an army component, and hospital component. A typical toxic faith type church specializes in the training and army components. They are quite focused on the mission of preaching the good news and setting the captives free. Often they will also embrace the importance for fellowship and relationship. But the relationships tend more and more to center around the mission and less and less on love, friendship, and healing. Very seldom will a toxic faith type church have a hospital component. Because the hospital is only for those who have just come to Christ and need healing and deliverance as part of the initial salvation process.

Typically, the counsel to church members with problems is short, simple, and ineffective. When a church member begins to talk about things like depression the classic answer is for them to serve more and then they will reap what they sow. When talk of burn-out rises up the answer is simply to pray more. Not praying to spend more time with God but rather to get 'refocused' on the job. When someone speaks of long-term problems creeping back, one is told those problems are not real because all things were made new in Christ Jesus. When someone talks about overwhelming temptations or problems, the quick answer is to 'read your Bible more'. The problem is that although all of these answers are good answers, but they are often not the complete answer.

The term 'toxic faith' obviously means a faith that is poisonous and dangerous to one's health. There can a point in the life of a church where if God's love, compassion, and mercy, are not focused on, then the good news can become the bad news. Jesus rebuked religious leaders of His day that *'travelled over land and sea to win a single convert, and when he becomes one, you make him twice as much a son of hell as you are'* (Matthew 23:15). Those leaders were very focused on the outer sacrifices, but they had neglected the issues of the heart. Jesus likened them to cups clean on the outside but filthy on the inside.

Because God is love His first priority is our relationships with Him. In toxic faith churches the emphasis is first on the performance and secondly on the fellowship with God. In John chapter 15, verse 8, Jesus stated that the Father was glorified by us bearing much fruit. But the route to becoming fruitful was to *'abide in Him.'* The process of fulfilling the greatest commandment (Mark 12:30), is to first love the Lord with all of our hearts. After that comes our mind and then our strength. To take that order backwards would be to say thirdly our outer sacrifices and endeavours, secondly our intellectual pursuit of Him, and first, as a foundation, our worship and prayers.

David said in Psalm 63, verse 3 that God's loving kindness is better than life itself. However, when a leader begins to start using people to build his or her empire, ministry changes from a sacrifice of joy to slavery. The issue is not whether we should live sacrificially. The answer is that giving, in whatever form, should come out of the joy in the Holy Spirit. It is better to give than to receive, and often we cannot really come into the joy of the Lord until we learn to start to pick up our cross daily. The danger of a toxic faith church, however, is that one is robbed of the intrinsic value God places on each of us.

God loves us so deeply for a multitude of reasons. He loves us because we are His creation. He loves us because He knows and understands our weaknesses and frailties. He loves us because we are made in His image. He loves us because Jesus has made us presentable to Him. He loves us because, if we have given Him our lives, we are now His Spirit-filled sons and daughters. In a toxic faith church, nevertheless, all of those reasons are left behind. We become valued and loved almost solely on the basis of how much we contribute and how hard we work.

This type of legalism, or a performance-based relationship with God, affects not only one's relationship with God but with one another. In classic examples of toxic faith churches, there is a clear 'pecking order'. Hence, someone with a visible profile such as a speaking ministry, becomes far more important and spiritual than a volunteer who sweeps the floor.

Not all callings are equal in importance, but all saints are of equal importance to God and should be to one another. Paul instructed the church in Corinth to no longer consider each other from a worldly viewpoint, but rather to regard each other as a new creation in Christ

(2 Corinthians 5:16–17). Jesus stated to His disciples that the greatest among them would be the servant of all. When the mission aspect of a church takes on a far greater importance that love, inevitably that church will turn more and more into a corporate system based on Darwin's theory of the survival of the fittest. In contrast to that worldly value system Paul wrote to the church in Corinth:

> '*On the contrary, those parts of the body that seem to be weaker are indispensable, and the parts that we think are less honorable we treat with special honor. And the parts that are unpresentable are treated with special modesty, while our presentable parts need no special treatment. But God has combined the members of the body and has given greater honor to the parts that lacked it, so that there should be no division in the body, but that its parts should have equal concern for each other. If one part suffers, every part suffers with it; if one part is honored, every part rejoices with it.*' (1 Corinthians 12:22–26)

The unravelling of a toxic faith church begins when core members come to the stage of either burn-out, or they need to go back into the hospital component for a season. As we have previously discussed in the book, the process of consecration and sanctification are lifelong. There are seasons in our lives where we become healthy enough to deal with long-standing issues that God wants to work on. Just as with some patients who vitally need an operation, if their system is too damaged or weak, they need to become stronger before the operation can be done. Often Satan has hooks in us that he will wait years and years before starting to manipulate, in order to bring the most damage to the Kingdom of God. When those seasons come on us we **do** need to read our Bibles more and to have faith and believe God's promises. But we also need spiritual families where transparency, love and compassion are of the highest value. When that atmosphere is not present, we often become like silly ostriches and bury our heads in the sand.

In the book *Toxic Faith; Understanding and Overcoming Religious Addiction*, the authors give the following definition of a religious addict:

> 'A religious addict is a person who uses faith to avoid reality and responsibility. Their intent is not to worship God, but to alter their perception of reality. They are driven by a perfectionism that causes them to attempt to earn favour with God through striving harder. Religion, not God, controls their lives.'[1]

Toxic faith churches like false religions, appeal to many because they can attempt to lose their problems in the system and its language. Members of these types of churches are discouraged from even speaking about issues and problems. When they do speak about personal problems they are given glib answers instead of love, healing, and encouragement. When members begin to speak out concerning real problems within the system they begin to be attacked with such classic labels as 'Jezebel' and 'rebellious'. David fearlessly prayed to God to search his heart and see if he had any wicked ways within him. The Bible is filled with prophetic messages from God who wanted to lovingly heal His people and house. God is never afraid to point out the hurts and sins within the body. His disappointment comes when we disbelieve so much in His compassion that we attempt to either hide the problem or justify ourselves.

We are called beyond a shadow of a doubt to be people of mission. God's Spirit is upon us to heal the broken hearts and proclaim liberty to the captives. We are called to heal the sick, cast out demons, and preach the good news. We have a mandate to minister to the widows and orphans, and to visit the prisoners. But, we are not only an army. We are family. We are not merely a corporation designed to put out a product as slickly and efficiently as possible. We are called to be people who love one another to such an extent that the world will know we are Christ's disciples. That love is to be based on God's incredible grace and compassion – an unearned gift given to each other. That does not mean that church discipline should never be invoked. But it means that not only in our strengths, but also in our weaknesses and times of difficulties, we should help carry one another's burdens. Jesus warned against leaders who continually operate in condemnation rather than grace and encouragement;

> *They tie up heavy loads, and lay them on men's shoulders; but they themselves are unwilling to move them with so much as a finger.'* (Matthew 23:4)

Note

1. Arterburn, Stephen, and Felton, Jack. Thomas Nelson Publishers: Nashville, 1991, pp. 31–46.

Chapter 9

The Classic Warning Signs

I have a friend, named John, who was formerly an avid basketball player. He is now unable to play because of so much damage to the tendons along the sides of the kneecap. When he had his knee opened up and examined by a specialist a few years back, the doctor was amazed at the deterioration. He asked John why he had waited so long to come in. The doctor explained that if he had taken care of his knee when the first symptoms appeared, years earlier, the damage would never have become this disabling. My friend had played for years with increasing pain but had never bothered about it. Finally his neglect had caused permanent damage. The only way John will be ever be able to play basketball again, short of a healing from God, is with very complicated and expensive surgery.

John's neglect of the early warning signs is a picture of many victim's experience with abusive leaders and systems. We will put up with pain until the point where the accumulated damage is overwhelming. Because a church is our immediate family in God the possibility of severe spiritual damage is a reality. For the sake of a diploma, or advancing a career, or a relationship, or in times of war, one can, for a limited time, put up with incredible stress. We may end up paying a cost for that stress but often the goal is worth the cost. The reward for ignoring basic warning signs of spiritual abuse for some is spiritual disaster. Until healed, the damage will almost always affect their relationship with God.

Many long-term victims of spiritual abuse never recover their first love for God. Often the only way out of complete disillusionment, is allowing God to do surgery on their hearts. But, often, by the time they reach that point, the heart can be so hardened by anger and pain that they feel unable to trust God again. To ignore any warning signs of increasing stress or pain over a long term is dangerous. But, perhaps, to ignore warning signs of spiritual abuse is the worst because of the consequences to the soul.

The following warning signs are common in abusive churches and systems. In almost any church there will be some areas where abuse takes place inadvertently. Mistakes will happen simply because all of us, including leaders, are human. If there had not been flaws in the early churches Paul would never have written many of his epistles. People who say they are looking for the perfect church are completely unrealistic. I tell people who refuse to commit to a church until they find the perfect one, that if they ever find onc they shouldn't go – they will just mess it up.

The point of this list is not to criticize every church. There will be a few signs of some of these in almost any church. In a truly abusive church, however, many of these will be in evidence. Often one is not able to see the abusive tendencies on the surface. Many people who are suffering abuse are sometimes so focused on the mission they don't really take note of the ongoing hurt. As the saying goes, they can't see the tree for staring so hard at the woods.

A visitor or new church member often cannot see the problems because they have not got beyond surface relationships. The new member may be caught up in the enthusiasm of the vision, or focused on the preaching or the worship. Just as one can visit a family for an evening and not discern the sexual abuse of a child, so it can be hard to really know a church family until you've lived with them for a while. Therein is the nature of the hook. One is usually not being abused until one has invested too much time and money to easily back out. And often those who are really involved but also recognize the problems, are scared of being a 'Jezebel' because of warnings from the leadership.

This is why it is so necessary to pray about where the Lord would have one fellowshiping. The same healthy attitudes one would want to apply to dating, should also apply to joining a church. Marriages based on a very short courtship can end up in disaster, whereas longer courtships give a better chance of knowing exactly whom you are marrying. The best way to really get to know a church is to visit some of the small groups and really sample some of the church members. If the sheep are healthy and happy the shepherds are doing their job.

1. Prevailing Attitudes of Elitism and/or Isolation

Fear tends to breed isolation. Christian 'cults' tend to be characterized by leaders calling for isolation from the rest of the body of Christ and society. Often controlling groups or people will show a disdain for others. Isolation, whether with individuals, families, or institutions, is usually a defence mechanism. When a group is living in fear they will resort to pride to legitimize their sense of the need for being distant from others. The root problem is not actually pride, although that may be part of the problem, but fear.

When the isolation is a distancing from other gospel-preaching, Bible-teaching churches, there could be a problem with pride. When the leaders begin to say things such as: 'forget everything you've learned about God before coming here' or 'we are the only ones with the true revelation' there is a major problem. The Bible is filled with instructions for having a loving regard for everyone who truly confesses Jesus Christ is Lord. The apostle Paul stated that no one can say 'Jesus is Lord' except by the Holy Spirit (1 Corinthians 12:3). In fact, Jesus stated that it is only in unity that the body of Christ will come into the fullness of

God's will (John 17:23). To cut off a regard for church history and other born again groups is in effect to try to divorce one's family and genealogy.

When group members are told to cut off all relationships outside the group, that should be considered a very serious warning sign. Paul said that we are in the world but not of the world. As Christians our values and practices are often at great odds with the world system. But we are also to be the spiritual lamps giving forth the true light of Jesus. As Jesus said:

> 'Neither do people light a lamp and put it under a bowl. Instead they put it on its stand, and it gives light to everyone in the house.' (Matthew 5:15)

Jesus Himself, while He never entered into sin, did spend time with sinners, including thieves and prostitutes. A Christian's chief relationships should be with other brothers and sisters in Christ, but if we completely cut ourself off from our neighbours and co-workers, how will they see the evidence of God's love in us and through us?

A major issue with some churches and cults is the fear of accountabiity. Proverbs chapter 18, verse 1 reads:

> 'He who separates himself seeks his own desire. He quarrels against all sound wisdom.' (NAS)

Spiritual pride can be a real problem in a church, but with a toxic faith type church the root cause of separation is fear of getting too close to others who might end up seeing faulty theology or abusive behaviour. In the same way, a family where a parent is sexually abusing the children often will avoid close contact with other families.

When one is rooted and grounded in God's love, one's sense of security and significance comes from our relationship with God and one another. When we derive our security and significance out of our performance we tend not to want to stand too close to others out of fear of looking less successful by comparison.

Another bad fruit from leaders maintaining attitudes of elitism is different standards between themselves and the people of the church. When this reaches an extreme, leaders will even feel that they have 'special license' from God to do what they want even if it is contrary to common biblical standards. This could be characterized by a 'us/them' mentality. Leaders in this scenario will often refer to themselves as 'God's anointed'. The church structure can soon have a hierarchy and pecking order the same as a secular corporation based on world values. The closer you get to the top of the pyramid the more 'spiritual' you are. Those lower down, or the 'sheep', are basically just there to support the ministry of the 'anointed ones'. This attitude is at great odds with Paul's statement in Ephesians 4:11–13. Paul states that the apostles, prophets, evangelists, and pastor/teachers are there to train and equip the church – the people, so that they can do the work of the ministry.

Leaders with attitudes of elitism will respond to questions concerning behavior and money by quoting the Bible; 'Don't touch God's anointed.' It should be noted that this is taking David's words out of context.

Sometimes in abusive churches the pastors will be angered if you don't refer to them by their title of 'pastor'. Jesus warned against a fixation on titles:

> *'And do not call anyone on earth "father," for you have one Father, and he is in heaven. Nor are you to be called "teacher," for you have one Teacher, the Christ.'*
>
> (Matthew 23:9–10)

God's delegated leaders should be honored as God-given gifts to the body of Christ, but, at the same time they should never hold themselves above the body, as that is God's place, not man's. Again, Jesus stated that His appointed leaders should not be as the Gentiles who love to lord their authority over people. Rather, they should emulate Him.

Although He was Lord and master He did not come to be served but to serve.

2. Leaders Practising 'Cursing' or Judging

One sad but classic example of elitism often seen in abusive churches, is what could be called 'cursing' those in the flock who either decide to leave, or who refuse to submit in questionable areas. In such situations, abusive leaders will pronounce judgments on those they perceive as disobedient. The curses will not be blatant, but will be cloaked in biblical terminology.

A common sort of curse would be a public proclamation that so and so has 'broken covenant' with the church or leadership. It is a deeply sad situation when someone must break off from a group of close friends that they have shared their lives with, and there are those who 'church hop'. But when a leader out of defensiveness, vindictiveness, or worry publicly attacks those who will not submit, it is cursing. This is wrong for two basic reasons. Jesus said *'do not judge'* in Matthew 7:1. He Himself is our judge. There are usually too many mixed motives in us to really offer righteous judgment. Those who do such things might quote the example of Peter with Ananias and Sapphira. From the text it seems Peter did not deal with this in a corporate meeting. He said it in a smaller one with probably just the other leaders present. Secondly, and more importantly, Peter was speaking out of a word of knowledge and in prophecy. The Lord did fulfill that word immediately. Peter's statement was not so much a judgment, as letting them know what God was doing.

Another pro 'cursing' argument some would make is to use Paul's order to disfellowship the man in the Corinthian church, who was in a sexual relationship with his step-mother (see 1 Corinthians chapter 5). What is of crucial importance in that situation is that the man was part of the church and living a lifestyle of blatant immorality. There is a three-step process Jesus gave for dealing with a brother, or sister, in clear sin such as immorality. Paul was not judging the man because of differences over leadership style. The whole of 1 Corinthians is on removing practising sinners from the church who claim to be Christians. There is no indication whatsoever of issues over control, abuse, or legalism. As a leader myself, I have had to in the past decide that a brother in fellowship was no longer welcome in our church. But that was after the first two steps of Matthew 18:15–16 had been followed. The man in that situation had been proven guilty in two or three cases of sex out of marriage and seducing single women in the fellowship.

The problems in pronouncing public judgments such as rebellion or jezebelic behavior are at least three-fold. First of all, as leaders, the people of the church really don't belong to us. Jesus is their true shepherd. They are really not under my authority but God's. If they are in sin against me then I should want to forgive them just as the Father wants to forgive me. The fact that some shepherds release such judgments into the public Christian arena is an indication that they are not really ministering out of a shepherd's heart. My heart for the sheep should be that if I cannot minister and lead them in a way that suits them then they can find a church and leader that does. My heart should be for them, not primarily concerned about building up my ministry.

Secondly, once that type of verdict or label goes public it will continue to haunt the person for a long time. Those sorts of judgments can prejudice people who have no need to even be aware of the basic conflict. Some counselors liken the resulting stress from such judgments to post-delayed stress syndrome that many Vietnam veterans have gone through. No matter how it is classified, when someone gives years of their life to a church and leaves in conflict, the pain can be traumatic, regardless of whether they are right or wrong. Even in worst-case scenarios where the culprit sheep truly is a rebel or a Jezebel, as a leader my prayer should be for them to find grace and healing. Rather than poison any future wells out of my own hurt, I should as much as possible be at peace with them, even if disfellowshiping was necessary. We need to remember to differentiate between the enemy, Satan, and his victims, who are sometimes deceived Christians.

The third problem in judging in such a way, is that none of us is really whole enough to take Jesus' place in doing that. Usually the church is like a precious child to the pastor. He has given his heart and soul to it. When someone tries to damage the church a pastor can become like a mother bear in attacking the one bad sheep in order to protect the rest. Leaders need to realize in such situations that although there may truly be sin on the part of that person, a vital question must be asked: 'why am I so deeply upset concerning this person?' Is it because of the potential damage they can bring to others, or am I worried that my empire might suffer? Am I responding in a Christ-like way or am I a slave in my need for success and respect in the eyes of others? Let's remember how Jesus behaved when His popularity was waning. He asked the twelve if they were going to leave also. There was no demand or attack on His part. As He said in John 14:30, Satan had no hold or hooks in Him which he could manipulate.

3. Denial of Freewill and Invasion of Privacy

Jesus died on the cross so that personal intimacy with the Father and Himself could be restored (John 17:3). Paul characterized the sons (and daughters) of God as those who are led by the Spirit. One of the most basic ways in which a Christian can be abused by a Christian leader is in the control or manipulation of their lives. A leader is called to preach and teach on things such as godly living, morality, and biblical ethics. In addition, church leaders need to warn people of the consequences of sin. In extreme situations of wanton disregard for biblical morality, leaders need to discipline church members, according to Matthew 18, verses

15–20. Where leadership can become controlling is when they begin to usurp the leading of the Holy Spirit in the life of the believer. Areas that tend to be controlled in unhealthy ways are:

- firmly controlling individuals choices in areas such as marriage, careers, etc.
- manipulating church members out of time and money
- auditing of finances
- manipulating members into assuming tasks and responsibilities, etc.

I am a firm believer in the principle of tithing. In fact, as a pastor, I do not believe someone really has joined a church family until they are tithing. But that must be a decision the individual makes of their own free will rather than by coercion or manipulation. Manipulation is the use of fear, flattery, and/or guilt to force a person to do something they are not inclined to do. We are all called as Christians to live sacrificially. But, as we have examined, God desires us to make choices out of love for Him and one another. God desires that we would give out of joy, not under compulsion or manipulation. As Paul wrote to the church in Rome:

> *'God has not given us a spirit of slavery, taking us back into fear again.'* (Romans 8:15)

Often, people in abusive systems are not allowed any privacy concerning their finances, marriage bed, and so on. In a healthy Christian marriage, for example, the sexual behavior of the couple is governed by wanting to please one another rather than using each other. In addition to biblical perspectives of what sexual immorality is and isn't, the couple govern their sexual practices out of their love and friendship for each other. As the apostle Paul stated *'the marriage bed is undefiled,'* but, it is also sacred. In some classic abusive churches pastorally appointed 'shepherds' pry into every area of their 'sheep's' lives. That sort of control is a definite invasion of privacy and a defilement of an area God sees as sacred.

Sometimes toxic faith type churches can be characterized by a serious lack of educated members. In such churches the leadership will have covertly discouraged people from having any confidence in their own understanding of the Bible. God has created all of us to operate not only as spiritual and physical beings but as intellectual ones as well. Paul stated that:

> '... the Bereans were of more noble character than the Thessalonians, for they received the message with great eagerness and examined the Scriptures every day to see if what Paul said was true.' (Acts 17:11)

There tends to be a certain 'mindlessness' amongst some toxic churches. People are strongly encouraged and manipulated to give and serve but not to really pursue Bible knowledge and use their brains. These types of churches can sometimes be referred to as 'cliché' churches: that is to say they reduce theology to trite religious sayings and favorite quotes of the pastor, and they use some scriptures as catch-alls, without understanding the context. On the other hand, a church composed primarily of blue-collar types or people in poverty by no means indicates an abusive church in itself.

4. Leadership Without Accountability

Those in leadership need to be free to lead, otherwise they are not really leaders. However, because a church is a family and not a hierarchy the church members should have the right to ask questions in humility. Often many pastors are themselves abused by church members who are anti-authority and controlled by pride. When the pendulum swings, however, we find leaders who take the attitude of lord as opposed to servant. Jesus came as a servant of all, but He clearly led His disciples and not vice versa.

In the context of love, commitment and humility, a church member should be free to ask questions. The operative word here is **ask**. Often people say 'I would like to ask you a question' but what they are really doing is demanding a compliance with their views or will. When a committed church member has questions they should be able to approach leadership and ask questions such as: 'why are we embracing this ministry? I don't understand', or 'I don't understand why this side of the church is so expensive to maintain, can you help me to understand the importance of the cost?' Healthy leaders who are intelligent want followers who are the same. Those leaders do not see it as an attack on their authority to answer questions asked in humility and at appropriate times. Unhealthy leaders are constantly afraid of being seen as mistaken. Their defence is to hold themselves aloof from the people and above reproach at all times.

The abuse of finances is probably one of the most noticeable abuses many churches commit. There are unfortunately many churches that do not handle money in a scrupulous manner. Obviously, for a leader to use his or her position to use church funds for themselves beyond their agreed salaries and benefits is theft. Many churches however, abuse leaders by demanding that their pastor work at a salary insufficient to support his family, according to the average wage of the church members. Paul said:

> *'The labourer is worthy of his hire.'*　　(1 Timothy 5:18)

Those who feel a pastor should not receive the equivalent of an executive with similar responsibilities in a secular job, will often say 'those in ministry should live by faith.' All Christians are to live by faith and all Christians are called to be servants of the gospel. Those that are called into full-time ministry are, according to the Bible *'worthy of double honour.'* Pastoring is one of the most stressful functions in existence. Members of a church should want to see the leaders who serve them amply provided for, so that relieved of financial stress, they can fully focus on the church.

The other side of the coin, however, are the wolves in

sheep's clothing. These can be leaders who see their ministry as a means to a financial end. Church finances need to be above-board. A healthy church should issue a financial statement to the members at least once a quarter. Once a month is probably safer. Leaders who see church income primarily as a way of extending the Kingdom of God have no qualms about stating in general terms in what directions the money is going. That does not mean that members have the right to demand changes in expenditures. Again, leaders need to be free to lead. And often those not really involved with a system or program cannot really understand all of the operating costs involved. But when church members have a good understanding that their money is financing the Kingdom of God, they have a greater incentive to really give liberally.

It is when leadership is misusing finances on an ongoing basis, that they handle the finances without accountability. They will cite heavy quotes regarding cleric/laity differences etc. When they are pressed they will resort to labels of rebellion and insubordination and act grieved. But this is the same sort of behavior a parent displays when abusing a child. They get huffy and defensive when troubling symptoms are noticed in their children by others. Where there is openness and transparency there is little room for the devil to come in.

5. Hazy Boundaries Between Serving God and Serving Leaders

In any relationship, including pastor and church member, love often involves gift-giving. Sometimes that gift may be money or things of value, and sometimes it may be service to that person. Demonstrations of love can turn to abuse when gifts of service are demanded.

Again, Jesus stated to His disciples that He did not come to be served but to serve. There is a call on leaders to lead, but with a servant's heart. He instructed the disciples not to be as the Gentiles who loved to lord it over people in their authority. When a pastor demands obsequious service and attitudes from followers he or she is clearly not truly representing Christ. This is an ongoing problem with many abusive churches. When words like 'we want to see a servant's heart demonstrated' are used to manipulate people into serving and giving in unhealthy ways, that is wrong.

In some Third World countries there is the ongoing problem of ethnocentricity. That is to say, the background cultural values often permeate the subsequent Christian culture. In some African churches for example, I have seen a pastor demand to be treated as a tribal chief would be treated in their native culture.

Christians should always show respect for the authority and responsibility God has called leaders to. But that can be taken out of proportion when a leader takes advantage of the followers. I have spoken with past members of abusive churches who were forced to go to their pastor's home to shovel snow or fix up basements. When a pastor demands that gifts be given him and service be rendered to him, abuse is definitely taking place.

6. Legalism and Condemnation

Often due to isolation and ignorance of the Bible, legalism is used by leaders as a way of keeping church members in check. The system in the old coal mining days was that the mining town would be totally owned by the company. Often the only work one could get was in the mines. But the company-owned stores and houses were priced to always keep the workers in debt to the company. The more in debt the worker became, the more of a slave he also became. As the old song went: 'I owe my soul to the company store.' This is a picture of churches that are primarily focused on the do's and don'ts. Since no one can ever be perfect, leadership will use condemnation as a hold over the people. People will come to church in fear and guilt rather than in joy. Instead of personal prayer being a time of love and communion it becomes a thing of religious drudgery. Instead of sacrificing out of joy, serving and giving become a legalistic system.

As discussed in a previous chapter there are areas in a believer's life that they must take responsibility for. Areas such as whether or not to drink wine, practise birth control, types of sex in marriage, home schooling, etc. These are, for the most part, 'grey areas'. They are not clearly spelled out as either right or wrong in the Bible. It is in these areas that the individual, or couple, must decide what the Bible says to them, what the Holy Spirit is saying, and what their personal convictions are. Paul said:

> '... all those who are led by the Spirit are the sons of God.'
> (Romans 8:14)

For a church leader to attempt to parentally control people in these areas is to rob people of their priesthood in Christ.

When a church begins to focus more on earning God's love than on what Jesus accomplished on the cross, legalism and the law will subtly but surely replace grace. The pulpit will be used increasingly to tie people up with condemnation. Rather than church members being encouraged to walk in the freedom of the Holy Spirit, the personal pursuit of outward perfection becomes a continual trap. Worship services go from being times of celebration of Jesus' victory, to sessions of religious soul flagellation.

Leaders are to promote and encourage God's people to live godly lifestyles. But the freedom to do so comes from the Holy Spirit. The Holy Spirit, God's presence, is the free gift of life because of the cross. Satan, being the accuser, constantly uses legalism to discourage and destroy us. When leaders constantly use the law to berate and tear down the sheep, Spirit-anointed encouragement is replaced by demonic condemnation. Isaiah prophesied of Jesus that He would not break the bent reed or blow out the flickering wick (Isaiah 42:3). Often people in a legalistic church stay for years in a 'Catch 22' syndrome with their sin. James spoke of confessing our sins to one another so that we might be healed. In a legalistic system however people are afraid to bring their bondages into the light. Instead of having an atmosphere of love, acceptance, and healing, a system of outward righteousness and inner turmoil will prevail. When one's group value is determined by being perfect, the group will always remember the problem rather than work towards the healing.

One definite warning sign of abuse is when a pastor takes the liberty of breaking the sacredness of the confessional. I am not speaking of turning over to officials the name of a murderer or child abuser as required by most laws in order to protect innocent people. I am referring to when the pastor takes what was shared in confidence in a counseling situation, and without any regard as to the heart and healing of the sinner, openly uses that person to make a point in a sermon. Usually it stems from the need of that pastor to impress the flock that he, or she, is superior and more holy than those he is ministering to. It is an attempt to produce fear in the church, in order to gain control. Obviously, that pastor's major concern is not for the sheep, no matter what sort of sermon he preaches.

7. Scapegoating and Denial Syndromes

The term 'scapegoating' comes from Leviticus, chapter 16. To make atonement to the Lord for the sins of the Hebrew people one goat would be killed and one released. The goat released out into the wilderness was a picture of us going free because Jesus paid the price for our sins.

Scapegoating can take on a whole new dimension when it is used as a form of denial. When one derives their significance and security from their performance, they will usually try to avoid confrontation or accountability. When they are confronted with a problem, usually they will immediately either resort to excuses or become defensive. Someone well developed in avoiding blame will often resort to scapegoating. That is to say it is never their fault. The blame always rests with someone else. This can accomplish two things. Firstly, the criticism is diverted away towards someone else. Secondly, the pent up frustration and anger over the situation can be unloaded on the scapegoat. This will temporarily defuse the situation.

I would like to borrow from Margaret Josephson Rinck, Ed.D. in helping to identify the process of scapegoating:

'In scapegoating, the family (or system) members all have a secret agreement: "we're ok, but so and so has or is a problem." Scapegoating is a psychological defence mechanism used to diffuse the anxiety in the system. (Remember, a system is an entity that has both content (ideas, role and definitions) and processes (that is, ways of doing things), and is complete in itself. In a way, a system is both the sum of its parts and greater than the sum of parts. It has a "life of its own" beyond its individual members.) [1]

As long as we're looking (or the organisation is looking) at the one or ones with the so-called "problem" we do not have to notice our own failings. The scapegoat takes our attention away from our failings, and bears the blame and shame for us. Whenever we see scapegoating in a system, whether it is a family or an organisation, we know there are deeper more basic problems which are being ignored.

Scapegoating is usually a very subtle process and many times, even the scapegoat may not realize it is happening. Sometimes the scapegoat does look like they are or have a problem and it appears that the others in the system are "only trying to help". Usually the scapegoat is someone who is very sensitive to the anxiety in the system.' [2]

Often systems (churches included) and families will use scapegoating rather than deal with hurting issues. Especially if admission of a problem could lead to danger of failure – losing sales, numbers, prestige, etc. A poor manager will blame his department's lack of growth on his salesmen, for not producing enough sales. Very often a pastor will blame the lack of growth in the church on the people for not giving, serving, or praying enough. Sometimes Christians have the habit of blaming Satan for all of their problems. The very next moment they will quote what John said:

'Greater is He who is in you than he who is in the world.'

(1 John 4:4)

When a system falls prey to scapegoating it becomes a vicious circle with everyone suspicious of everyone else. People become afraid to ask for help or confess problems. The 'weak link' is usually attacked for lack of commitment and faith. The biggest problem with a church caught up in scapegoating is that healing and wholeness become rare. And the more the tension grows as Satan and life's pressures twist the screws, the more sick the members become. When someone high up becomes burnt out and needs a break, they are labeled as 'back-slidden' or 'losing faith'. Because the leadership is addicted to success, the sheep are used by the shepherds and then branded as outcasts when they cannot perform. Scapegoating is often the number one problem of toxic faith type churches. Members are used as a commodity to obtain the leadership's desires.

As we saw earlier, often the core people caught up in abusive churches are religious addicts. When a church, from the leadership on down, is comprised of mainly religious addicts Jesus becomes their drug or tool for denial. Their personal relationship with God is often slight. Prayer and worship are seen as tools rather than communication.

8. A Continuous Turnover of Leaders and Staff

This last area of warning is one that is perhaps the most noticeable to those who may not be involved in the core of the church. This is where periodically, key leaders underneath the senior leader either leave or are fired. These events usually lack clear, coherent explanations, or are surrounded by accusations that usually go beyond the known character of the departing leader. The basic reason is almost always the same; the leader or staff person, has either confronted the abusive senior leader or has made it clear that he, or she, can no longer support an abusive system.

To quote the famous saying attributed to the actor W.C. Fields:

'You can fool some of the people all of the time, all of the people some of the time, but you can't fool all of the people all of the time.'

Most smart leaders, including abusive ones, desire to have the very best help they can get. The exception, of course, is extremely insecure leaders who are easily threatened by those more gifted or whole than themselves. These leaders will seldom put strong, gifted, or whole leaders into responsible positions as they are very afraid of being seen in a bad light. They are characterized by having a staff made up mostly of 'yes' men – leaders who will never challenge them, even in the context of love and respect. The quality of the support leadership and staff, is usually a good indicator as to the health of the senior leadership. Like attracts like. Unhealthy leaders mainly attract other unhealthy people.

Smart leaders, however, want the very best workers they can get. Therein lies the problem. Usually support leaders who are gifted and mature, will soon begin to notice abusive tendencies being propagated by the senior leader. True shepherds will be concerned for not only the size of the flock, but the condition of the individual sheep. As they notice a growing tendency of the sheep being 'used' to facilitate the senior leader's vision they will, at least in the context of love and humility, begin to raise questions to the leader.

The initial tendency is for the leader to smooth over the

problems. The leader will say that inevitably some people just do not fit into a highly visionary church. After all, you can't make an omelette without cracking a few eggs. Anyway there is no such thing as a perfect church. And usually, they can move into scapegoating and point out the problems of that particular brother or sister in question. Usually, because the sub-leaders do love and respect the senior leader, they will then accept the explanations and either dismiss their questions or put them on the back burner.

As the cycle goes, however, usually abusive syndromes get a whole lot worse before anyone seriously wants to deal with the issues. The problems, however, not only do not disappear, but they get a whole lot more widespread and developed. Soon it is not just a few people being hurt, but more and more committed core people making a noise and suffering burn-out. It is usually at this point that those who are smart enough and experienced enough, will no longer accept the labeling and scapegoating being done by the senior leader. An unhealthy shepherd merely beats the sheep when they are bleating and stammering. A healthy shepherd wants to know why they are upset and will correct the problems. It is at this point that those strong and mature sub-leaders and staff, will end up leaving the church. They have come to the point of realizing that the senior leader will neither face the reality of the problems, nor implement change where needed. Those leaders will then leave rather than continue to contribute to a toxic faith system. On the part of the senior leader, he will get rid of those sub-leaders as quickly as possible as they, in his mind, pose a serious threat to the success of his mission, which is personal success. Usually, the more visibility the departing leader had, the greater will be the attack launched by the senior leader.

This scenario is not entirely exclusive to toxic faith type churches. There can be senior leaders who would never abuse the people but are so controlled by fear and insecurity that they cannot stand for others to be in the limelight. In these cases the abuse is usually limited to those within the circle of central pastoral leadership. It is still, none the less, a serious indicator of unhealthy leadership. Healthy people cultivate healthy relationships. Healthy church leaders raise up healthy churches. Unhealthy leaders tend to raise up unhealthy disciples. Unhealthy leaders striving for outward success will usually attract religious addicts of the same make-up as themselves. They will attract others who want to use ministry and religion as a drug to cover up their inner problems and tensions. Most of the time, however, this scenario will take place among churches involved in long-term spiritual abuse.

Notes

1. Schaef, A.W. and Fassel D., *The Addictive Organisations*, Harper and Row: San Francisco, 1988, p. 60.
2. Richardson, Ronald W., *Family Ties that Bind*, International Self-Counsel Press Ltd: Seattle, 1987, p. 64.

Chapter 10

The Abuse of Leaders

slander – the utterance of false charges or misrepresentations which defame and damage another's reputation.

gossip – a person who habitually reveals personal or sensational facts.

(Webster's New Collegiate Dictionary, 1977)

manipulation – the subtle, or not so subtle, use of fear, flattery, or guilt to force someone to do what they do not want to do. (The author)

Normally, when we think of spiritual abuse we picture a heavy-handed and controlling leader ministering out of blind ambition or, perhaps, deep insecurity. In actuality, however, there is a more wide-spread problem of abuse of church leaders by the people, than the other way round. This does not take away from the realities of the hurts suffered by those who have submitted to abusive leaders, which is the thrust of this book. The opposite problem, nevertheless, needs to be addressed because hurting people who don't get healed, invariably, end up hurting others, whether they are leaders or followers.

God's Authority; Both Inherent *and* Delegated!

We, as Christians, have been bought with a price. Our very lives do not belong to ourselves anymore, but to God (1 Corinthians 6:19–20). When we lay down our rights to self-determine our own wills, we honor God's delegated authority. In our western world, we usually think of God's authority over our lives as purely inherent. God's inherent authority is directly from Him to us. It may come to us through the Bible, the leading of the Holy Spirit, or preaching, or prayer, but it is God's clear will for us.

God also exercises His will for our lives in a secondary way through His delegated authority. That is, through leaders, pastors, overseers, bishops, etc. through which He leads His church. Obviously, leaders being human, there is, unfortunately, room for misuse of God-given authority or else we would not need books such as this. But, as the saying goes, we can not throw out the baby with the bath water. In the previous chapter we examined certain warning signs that can be key indicators of when church leaders are overstepping their boundaries and moving into control and abuse. Although this is a very real problem, just as real a problem are Christians who refuse to allow God's delegated authorities to lead the church.

The problem of churches abusing pastors, or leaders, is essentially a two-fold problem. Firstly, the two current generations under sixty years of age tend to be extremely rebellious. The sixties generation, as a matter of fact, specialized in rebellion. Rebellion of all standards and authorities. Whether it was culturally, politically, or morally, rebellion was the standard of the decade. Although it is less overt and focused, the children of sixties parents grew up and now live in an inherited state of rebellion. The rebellion of the 1980s and 1990s is usually not dressed up in politics and causes as much as the 1960s. It is more of a plain, blatant, and naked rebellion of selfishness.

The second primary reason church members abuse, leaders is really the same reason, but disguised with faulty theology and misapplied spirituality. That is to say many Christians simply do not understand the Kingdom of God is a monarchy rather than a democracy. Jesus never said to seek to do with your whole heart what we think best. He said to *'seek first the Kingdom of God and His righteousness.'* An English pastor I know used the following comparison to describe the state of many Christians with regard to spiritual authority. He described how many English people love the tradition of monarchy in their country. They loved the historical pomp and ceremony surrounding the queen and the royal family. They loved the symbolism and the idea of a country being represented by a royal person or family. However, they also love their democracy and parliamentary procedure. He went on to say the people of England are much like many churches. The people want both democracy and a monarchy. And just like England, we can end up with a royal leader (God) who tends to be more symbolic than authoritative in deciding our wills.

The word 'monarch', the Latin phrase we use for king, or queen, is made up of two words. *'Mon'* means 'one' as is one and only one; the word *'arch'* means 'ruler' or 'chief'. In essence, when Jesus said to seek first the Kingdom of God, He was emphasizing the importance of seeking God's will for your life, rather than merely **doing your own thing** even though you may be saved and going to heaven.

As the prophet Samuel said to King Saul: *'Your rebellion is as witchcraft.'* In that scenario Saul had disregarded God's authority delegated to Samuel. Saul had been more controlled by his own desires to preserve the best of the spoils of war for himself. In the book of James, James contrasts wisdom from above with fleshly wisdom which is *'earthly, natural, and demonic'* (James 3:15, NASB). James characterizes that wisdom as being rooted in jealousy, selfish ambition, and arrogance. In the Kingdom of God the path to fulfillment is to die to self. In our natural (carnal) way of thinking we want to place ourselves and our desires ahead of others. When a leader is primarily motivated by self-ishness and ambition the fruit can be abuse of the church. When a church member is primarily motivated by selfish ambition the result can be abuse of the leadership.

A classic biblical picture of honoring delegated authority is Jesus and John the Baptist. John, in preparation for the coming of Jesus, was baptizing people for the repentance of sins. One day Jesus Himself showed up on the scene. He had joined the crowd and wanted to be baptized by John. John, by the Spirit, recognized Him as the Messiah. John promptly protested. In fact he tried to prevent it (Matthew 3:13–17). He exclaimed, *'I have need to be baptised by You, and do You come to me?'* Jesus' response is critical in understanding delegated authority. He replied to John, *'Permit it at this time, for in this way it is fitting for us to fulfil all righteousness.'*

Jesus as the spotless, sinless, perfect sacrificial Lamb of God had no sin in His life. John was baptizing people for 'repentance of sins'. Why would Jesus want to be baptized by John when He had no sin? The answer is that Jesus understood delegated authority. Jesus always was the only begotten Son of God. In the beginning He was not only with God but God (John 1:1). But, He recognized not only the Father's inherent authority over His life but also His dele-gated authority over His life. He honored the authority of Joseph and Mary as a boy and young man. Luke 2:52 says that *'Jesus grew in wisdom and stature, and in favor with God and men.'* He lived His life in a way that was pleasing both to the Father and to His human parents. When it came time to begin His ministry in earnest, He began by recognizing the Father's delegated authority upon John the Baptist. It wasn't that Jesus needed to repent of any personal sins because He simply didn't have any, but Jesus, even though He was the Begotten Son of God recognized that John was still the Father's chief spokesmen for the hour.

Here is one of the critical reasons for many gifted but frustrated people in some churches. Many want authority but refuse to recognize authority. A basic rule in the King-dom of God, and in fact in all of life, is you cannot really receive authority until you first recognize God's authority. Jesus did recognize the delegated authority on John. So rather than minister to John He insisted that John baptize Him so that 'all righteousness' could be fulfilled. It was after Jesus' demonstration of humility that the Father spoke stating how pleased He was with His Son. It was after the submission to John's ministry that the Holy Spirit came on Jesus as a dove and anointed Him for the work soon to come. The dove is symbolic of power through peace. James stated that wisdom from above is pure and peaceable. Whereas human wisdom, from ambition and striving, is argumentative and arrogant. The source of human wisdom is always self and pride of self. Saul's rebellion against Samuel's delegated authority was motivated by self.

Is there a time to leave an abusive church or religious system? Definitely! When the warning bells begin to go off and you realize that to stay is going to bring destruction, that's the time to move on. But when we read of David having to run from King Saul it is important to note two things. Firstly, He always honored Saul's authority and anointing. David did not leave until Saul began to seriously try to kill him. Years later, when Saul and his army were pursuing David in the wilderness, David twice had the opportunity to kill Saul. Many would argue, in fact some of David's men did, that David had every right to kill Saul (1 Samuel 24:4–7). David had never done anything against Saul, and after all Samuel the great prophet had anointed David as the true king over Israel. But David's response was that there was no way he would harm God's anointed. Secondly, when David did run from Saul he did not try to breed rebellion. He never did try to usurp his authority. In fact, when David found out later on that Saul and Jonathan were dead, he mourned them both deeply. David, obviously saw the flaws in Saul as a man and a leader. But even more than that, David honored the authority and anointing from God on Saul. There is a time when to leave a church is the only option. But care needs to be taken that our attempts at self-preservation do not turn into rebellion against God, whether direct or indirect.

Latent Rebellion

One of the biggest areas of abuse of leaders is what could be called latent, or passive, rebellion. Passive rebellion is when an individual is not fighting authority overtly in clearly defined ways but rather, they are continually whittling away at a leader's authority in small, subtle, covert ways. The chief characteristic, perhaps, of latent rebellion, is a continual and subtle misuse of the tongue. Someone caught up in latent rebellion tends to always be questioning authority. Not in open, clearly defined questions but in continual, subtle criticism and comments. Usually, those involved in passive rebellion towards a church leader will posture their rebellion in spiritual appearances. So, they will ask so-called theological questions regarding every step the leadership takes. Certainly, the whole body should have access to ask questions and have legitimate discussions regarding teaching, as Paul noted in the Berean church (Acts 17:10–11). And as previously pointed out, committed church members should be able to, in humility, ask questions of leaders concerning church direction and decisions. What we are addressing here, however, is an individual who is more concerned with fault-finding than with real issues and questions.

Often those involved in latent rebellion will be highly involved in near-leadership functions, such as intercessory prayer, worship, leading home groups, etc. Usually those around them pick up after a while that everyone else's ministry is a little off but theirs. They will use their 'special knowledge and insights' to casually question and effectually undermine everyone over them in authority. Under the cover of 'needing to warn people to pray for the pastor' they will spend hours on the phone gossiping, or writing slanderous letters about the pastor. When questioned concerning their behavior they will vigorously defend themselves by claiming to be the pastor's biggest supporter and that they just want to 'watch out for him spiritually'. In fact, many will claim God has called them to be a 'watchman' for the pastor. If Bible knowledge or theology is their weapon, they will often spend time on Sundays after the service with other 'concerned' members talking at length about how the message was 'okay – but there were a few points of "concern" they have.'

It needs to be noted that slander and gossip are serious sins. In fact, Jesus listed slander in the same category as murder and adultery (Mark 7:21–23). *'All these evil things proceed from within and defile,'* Jesus stated. When a person, including a Christian, is reduced to little more than continually grumbling and being contentious, the real problem lies within their heart. *'Do all things without grumbling or disputing,'* Paul commanded the church at Philippi (Philippians 2:14, NASB). The writer of Hebrews instructed the Christians to:

> *'Obey your leaders, and submit to them; for they keep watch over your souls, as those who will give an account. Let them do this with joy and not with grief, for this would be unprofitable for you.'* (Hebrews 13:17, NASB)

Clearly, according to both the book of Philippians and Hebrews, both latent and obvious rebellion towards church leaders is a real sin in the eyes of God. James wrote concerning improper use of the tongue:

> *'With the tongue we praise our Lord and Father, and with it we curse men, who have been made in God's likeness. Out of the same mouth comes praise and cursing. My brothers, this should not be. Can both fresh water and salt water flow from the same spring? My brothers, can a fig tree bear olives, or a grapevine bear figs? Neither can a salt spring produce fresh water. Who is wise and understanding among you? Let him show it by his good life, by deeds done in the humility that comes from wisdom. But if you harbor bitter envy and selfish*

ambition in your hearts, do not boast about it or deny the truth. Such "wisdom" does not come down from heaven but is earthly, unspiritual, of the devil. For where you have envy and selfish ambition, there you find disorder and every evil practice. But the wisdom that comes from heaven is first of all pure; then peace-loving, considerate, submissive, full of mercy and good fruit, impartial and sincere.'

(James 3:9–17)

Sin is Satan's legal domain. When church members practice gossip and slander, grumbling and contentiousness, no matter what the excuse, legal access is given to Satan. What this means is that open doors to the working of the enemy exist in many churches because of latent rebellion. I have noticed over the last 15 years of international ministry that many pastors, their wives and families, seem to suffer an inordinate amount of sickness. This is often due to the moral problems such as stress, generational curses, warfare and bad eating habits that we all face. But I am convinced that to some degree many leaders and their families suffer needlessly because some church members are sinning against their God-given leaders. Even when physical illness is not in evidence, many leaders and their spouses have almost entirely lost their joy in serving the body of Christ, due to the relentless criticism within the church family which attacks them at almost every turn.

As Hebrews states, it is not profitable to cause grief to those who lead. In fact, it is sin. As Jesus and James point out, the root cause for continual misuse of the tongue is bitterness, jealousy, and selfish ambition deep within the heart. There are those who profess to be Christian, but are actually practising jezebelic behavior. They are attempting to usurp God-given leadership purely to fulfill their own personal agenda, fueled by demonic fires of ambition. Those in latent rebellion are consistent with the working of the Jezebel spirit in that they will appear to be very spiritual, but their hearts and the fruit of their lips result in division and selfishness.

Rebellion and Scapegoating

In the previous chapter we examined the syndrome of scapegoating by some leaders. This is the process of casting blame at others in order to diffuse anger and hide one's own problems. This defence mechanism can also be practised by church members as well as leaders. To define it simply we would say that many people always lay the blame for their problems at the door of the nearest authority figure. We see this in liberal politics where the conservative government is always the cause of life's problems and personal responsibility is rarely, if ever, addressed. Christians involved in this type of rebellion, simply do not want any personal accountability.

The word 'accountability' has almost become a term many pastors are afraid to use because of the abuses in toxic faith churches. But again, the baby cannot be thrown out with the bath-water. Christianity, at least from a biblical perspective, is lived out in the context of relationships. Healthy relationships are a two-way street. We derive strength and encouragement from relationships but we can also receive loving correction and warnings. Part of a pastor's or elder's job description, is to not only encourage the flock but to bring warnings, correction, and even discipline when necessary. Often when a leader does fulfill the more unpleasant side of his function the critics say 'that's not very reflective of Jesus.' Those sort of comments come from a half-baked knowledge of God's word. It was Jesus, in Matthew 18, who laid down a three-step process for dealing with serious sin within the church. The third step is expulsion from the gathering of the local church. Paul, as well, stated in 1 Corinthians 5:11:

> '... you must not associate with anyone who calls himself a brother but is sexually immoral or greedy, an idolater or a slanderer, a drunkard or a swindler. With such a man do not even eat.'

Obviously, accountability is an area that leaders can in

unbiblical, or anti-biblical ways, abuse a church member's life. What is far more common, though, is for church members to lash out at leaders and blame them for problems in their personal life or the life of a church. 'You know, if Jim really preached the word we would grow like some of the other churches' or 'Well, if pastor Jim really cared about me I would not be having these problems.' People who resort to such statements usually regard convicting preaching or attempts at personal pastoral oversight as 'meddling'. But when the problems stemming from personal sin begin to escalate, suddenly it is because the 'pastor doesn't care'.

For sure there are some in senior leadership roles who should not be there, and, just as there is no such thing as a perfect church there is also no such thing as a perfect pastor. It is in the working out, however, between imperfect human beings that God has ordained true love, grace, and mercy to flourish. True maturity in this realm is not when we arrive at a legalistic perfection because complete holiness is not possible. True maturity is when we begin to start 'owning our problems' and in a place of humility want to repent and change our ways by God's grace. It is all too easy to blame authority figures for our problems. It is an altogether different thing to take responsibility and see how we can change. Often the choice in life is either to change, or to be changed!

Love Asks, Not Demands

Another problematic area where pastors are quite often abused is when the people of the church demand, rather than ask for ministry. When considering classic abuse we think of a leader who holds himself above the people, using them rather than ministering to them with a servant's heart. The flip side of that is when members of a church treat the pastor or leaders as little more than hired servants.

A common example that probably every pastor has encountered, are the midnight phone calls of desperation.

The common scenario is a church member or couple that have been living with issues such as the sin of bitterness and/ or anger towards each other for years. The pastor has tried to coax the couple into counseling or at least facing the reality of their situation many times. But now at 11.00 at night, the pastor has to come over and straighten out 'the problem'. This is a pastorally abusive situation simply because the couple have resisted every attempt from the pastor to bring correction, but now that the situation is explosive he, or she, must come at once and magically fix 'the problem'. No thought is given to the fact that the typical pastor works a minimum of 60–70 hours per week and is entitled to a peaceable evening at home with his family. It is abusive because the couple are demanding on their terms, a solution that will turn out to be a band aid because they do not want to deal with the real problem – their hearts. It is abusive because if the pastor is too tired, or has too much sense to jump when they call, they will spread the story that the pastor does not really 'love them' enough to reach out to them. In discussing pride versus humility it must be noted that many are willing to admit that they have a problem but are unwilling to take ownership of their problem. Often these types are 'codependent'. They are not so much interested in getting healed as they are using their problem to get attention. If the pastor is smart enough to avoid the manipulation then he becomes labeled as 'uncaring'.

One friend of mine started out in pastoring a small church in Texas. The home he and his wife lived in was owned by the church and considered part of the pastoral pay package. He and his wife came home one day to find two ladies from the church going through their personal belongings in the bedroom. They thought they had a right to know about their possessions since the church paid their salary.

The pastor and his family of the Baptist church I was saved in, were often plagued by phone calls at all hours of the day and night. Sometimes the phone calls were normal or ministry related, but often they were simply church members who wanted phone numbers. No thought was given to the fact that they were a family too, and had a right not to be treated as an all-hours information service for the church.

Perhaps some of the most consistent abuse takes place in charismatic and Pentecostal churches where some members feel they have the 'word of the Lord' for the church's direction. They believe that their spiritual perception somehow completely overrides the pastor's authority and commission from God to lead. Somehow these wannabe Samuels and Elijahs forget that Paul said prophecy is to encourage, strengthen, and edify: not to control or manipulate. The classic response when the pastor does not completely adhere to their untested word is that the pastor is 'quenching the Holy Spirit'.

Manipulation of Leaders

Many of us, whether knowingly or not, practise the subtle art of manipulation. In general, manipulation involves the use of fear, flattery, or guilt to coerce someone to do what we want when they really do not want to do it. A classic example is an unscrupulous used car salesman who fawns over ignorant customers. He will compliment them on how discerning they are. Only afterwards when the customer has paid way too much for way too little, and tries to get the dealer to take care of the problems does it become obvious that it was all flattery designed to 'hook the fish'. That would be an example of very obvious manipulation on the part of the manipulator. Another such example would be when an employer assigns a highly unpleasant task that was not part of the initial job description. You are then told either do it or 'you're fired'. Sometimes, however, manipulation can be an unconscious tactic. Some people are simply so encouraging to be around, that we find ourselves doing favors for them we cannot really afford to do. They do not necessarily mean to use their encouragement in an unhealthy way to take advantage over us. It's just that they are feeding us in an area where we may be very lacking, such as affection and encouragement.

Lovers and good friends will often use affection to fulfill each other's needs and desires. A wife will cook her husband's favorite meal before telling him that she would very much like the interior of the house repainted. Men will quite often take a woman out for an expensive dinner in the hope of a night of romance. Often in these sort of situations, manipulation is not necessarily evil. In fact it can be part of the understood social rules that are expected and enjoyed in certain types of relationships and friendships. Where manipulation does become unhealthy, is when for example, it is a continual device employed by an authority figure to do things either against our better judgement, or at too great a personal sacrifice. Manipulation is evil when the manipulator is operating without any real regard for the person he, or she, is manipulating.

Pastors of small churches, under 200 people or so, tend to be the targets of manipulation from some of the members. A very classic example is when a long-standing church receives a new pastor. Sooner or later that new pastor will begin to implement changes. Some of the changes may be minor, eventually some major ones will be put into effect. This should be expected since God gives us different personalities and works through each of us differently. There will be a group among that church who feel that the way things have been, is the way things always should be. Sooner or later a key tither of that group will approach the pastor and say 'you know if you keep going the way you are it will affect the offerings.' What they are really saying is 'you better do what I want or I will no longer support the church financially, and you know the church needs my money.' Another classic manipulation, along the same lines, will be the warning, 'if you go with this new vision probably some are going to leave the church.' What they are actually saying is, 'I and my friends are going to fight you tooth and nail over this issue and if you win, you will still lose because we will then leave the church.' In both situations the manipulators are neither whole enough or mature enough to sit down and humbly ask why the pastor is taking the flock in the direction they are. And if they do understand, but still persist in manipulation, basically it is an indicator of rebellion.

Again, church members should have the right to ask questions in humility. A healthy leader will want his followers to fully understand why they are embarking in a fresh direction. An informed follower usually will stick to his resolve because they fully understand why they are making sacrifices. But where there is rebellion, whether overt or latent, there is the strong hold of selfishness that tends to rule the heart. As previously mentioned this sort of selfishness can lead to real sin in fighting against God's delegated authority.

We are often the unwilling victims of one another's abuses and manipulations, whether we are in leadership or not. The point in mentioning these examples is to show that abuse is unfortunately not only all too common but it also is a two-way street. To lay down one's life as the good shepherd for the sheep is a godly thing. Being human, sometimes leaders fall prey to heavy handedness and manipulation. But we the sheep, also being human, often fall prey to ignoring the honor and delegated authority that go with the calling, and abuse those gifts God has given us in love.

Chapter 11

Lethal Love – Shame

'The most spiritual human beings, assuming they are the most courageous, also experience by far the most painful tragedies: but it is precisely for this reason that they honor life, because it brings against them its most formidable weapons.'

(Friedrich Nietzsche: 1844–1900
German Philosopher)

One of the most painful effects of long-term spiritual abuse is shame. Shame, unlike guilt over a specific sin or mistake, is the general deep-down feeling of depravity and unworthiness. The true crime of spiritual abuse of born again Christians is that to a large degree the righteousness Jesus died to give us instead of our shame is almost stolen from the victim. The ensuing aftermath of abuse often leaves people floundering in a mire of shame and hopelessness. I would like to use this chapter to focus on the dilemma of shame in relationship to toxic faith churches and victims.

A few years ago there was a wonderful book published called, *All I Really Need To Know I Learned In Kindergarten*. The author captured the public's attention when he cleverly described the creed he lived by, and the simple rules for life he followed:

'All I need to know, and how to live, and what to do, and how to be, I learned in kindergarten.' [1]

Kindergarten was the place where you learned to share everything, play fair, and not hit people, to put things back where you found them, and to hold hands and stick together. You learned to say sorry when you hurt somebody and not to take things that weren't yours and to wash your hands before you eat. These simple rules for living were refreshing to read again and reminded us of how uncomplicated life once was.

Unfortunately, life isn't that elementary. These aren't the only edicts children learn when they enter kindergarten. They experience, possibly for the first time, that life isn't so fair, that people don't share everything, and don't say they are sorry if they've hurt you. Life can all of a sudden become difficult or overwhelming when outsiders first notice our unique family traits and features.

Most of us can recall the excruciating moment when we were teased by our friends and called four-eyes, brace-face or carrot-top. Maybe you were hurt and even confused when someone made fun of your big ears, or the mole on your chin when all along you thought you looked just fine. Perhaps you were called names because you were too short or too tall or too smart or not smart enough. Whatever your predicament, being teased for **who** you were felt humiliating and embarrassing. Returning insult for insult or yelling, 'sticks and stones may break my bones, but words can never hurt me!', couldn't take the sting out of their words. We learned, as early as kindergarten, that cruel words cut deep and can leave life-long scars.

That old familiar feeling, the one that stings and hurts and cuts deep into our being, is called shame. Shame is a soul-deep sense that there is something uniquely and hopelessly wrong with **me**. I believe somehow that I am flawed or worthless and quite possibly a mistake. When you experience shame, you feel isolated and alienated from others. It is as if you are standing alone on one side of a broken bridge while everyone else in the world stares at you from the other side of the bridge. Shame symptoms include beliefs, emotions and behaviors that display the underlying pain that comes from seeing ourselves as eternally separated from others.[2]

Feeling shamed is very different from being guilty. We interchange these words in our conversation all the time. For example, 'I feel guilty that I didn't return my library book on time.' Or, 'I feel guilty that I got caught driving over the speed limit.' What we experience in both of these circumstances is shame, not guilt. True moral guilt is always the result of violating God's standards. Guilt says I made a mistake, I did something wrong. Shame on the other hand says I am a mistake, there is something wrong with me. Feeling shame is the most poignant experience of the self by the self, whether felt in humiliation or cowardice, or in a sense of failure to cope successfully with challenge. Shame is a wound felt on the inside, dividing us both from ourselves and from one another.[3]

When we violate God's law, when we are guilty, we can ask for forgiveness. He then wipes the slate clean. It's that simple. He remembers it no more. No strings attached. I believe we are so accustomed to feeling so much shame, we can hardly differentiate between the two; did I make a mistake or am I a mistake? Recently, I was standing in front of our municipal judge paying a traffic ticket. I had to say out loud and for the record, 'I am guilty.' And I was, I broke the law. However, I did not think or feel that I was a lesser human being because of it. I make a mistake. That's it. I wasn't obligated to the Judge, to myself or to our Heavenly Judge to berate and shame myself for being a mistake. (It was just my luck however, to be pulled over in front of church Easter morning for the entire world to see!)

It is a sad fact of life that in our families and in our churches, we have experienced an overdose of shame. We are bombarded with messages every day that communicate we are not good enough, perfect enough or smart enough. We wake up every morning to face the day and prove to the world (our bosses, our pastors, our peers) that we can do 'it' better. Even though we're grown, we are like little children who vie for their parents' attention and yell, 'Hey dad, look at me!' Somewhere deep in our memory banks, I think we greet each day hoping or wishing, 'I want to be perfect!' Because, if we were perfect, if we could do 'it' perfectly, we would never have to experience the painful feeling of shame.

One of the reasons we are so accustomed to and accept living a shame-filled life, is that we've had a lot of time to practice.

> *'In the very beginning God created male and female in his own image, in the image of God he created them; and it was very good.'*

I often wonder what it was like to see the reflection and likeness of God when you looked in the mirror. The only image Adam and Eve could see or ever knew was the *Imago Dei*, the image of God. Can you imagine having only unconditional love and absolute respect for yourself when you looked at your reflection? To be perfectly transparent and open before the Father, and each other, without having to hide or defend yourself? It's no wonder in the beginning when man and his wife were both naked, they felt no shame. The Lord was reflecting His message, His truth about who they were into their very beings.

> *'Now the serpent was more crafty than any of the wild animals the Lord God had made. He said to the woman, "Did God really say, 'You must not eat from any tree in the garden?'"*
>
> *The woman said to the serpent, "We may eat fruit from the trees in the garden, but God did say, 'You must not eat fruit from the tree that is in the middle of the garden, and you must not touch it, or you will die.'"*
>
> *"You will not surely die," the serpent said to the woman. "For God knows that when you eat of it your eyes will be opened, and you will be like God, **knowing good and evil**."*
>
> *When the woman saw that the fruit of the tree was good for food and pleasing to the eye, and also desirable for*

gaining wisdom, she took some and ate it. She also gave some to her husband, who was with her, and he ate it. Then the eyes of both of them were opened, and they realized they were naked; so they sewed fig leaves together and made coverings for themselves.

The man and his wife heard the sound of the Lord God as he was walking in the garden in the cool of the day, and they hid form the Lord God among the trees of the garden. But the Lord God called to the man, "Where are you?"

He answered, "I heard you in the garden, and I was afraid because I was naked, so I hid." '   (Genesis 3:1–10)

Adam and Eve's relationship with the Lord was changed forever. They were no longer transparent and open, they were exposed and vulnerable, full of fear and shame. They knew they were guilty for breaking God's only requirement of them.

For the very first time, they saw themselves as something other than God's perfect reflection. They could see both the good and the evil in themselves, and in each other. Their beliefs about who they were changed, and so therefore, did their feelings. As Adam and Eve abandoned God, they were, in turn, abandoned by God. It was out of this original abandonment that the shame base for the rest of humanity was established. The experience of abandonment means that the person who is abandoned is left with the feeling of valuelessness. Rejection is a death experience. Yet, while God's abandonment of us in judgment is always relative (God clothed Adam and Eve even as they were expelled from Eden), it feels absolute to us.[4]

Since we now know we are separated from God's perfect reflection, we've learned (and quite well I might add) to cover up our imperfections. We are well trained, like an Olympic athlete, to defend and blame and protect our flawed selves at all costs. Even the very thought of becoming intimate, transparent, or to trust another person with my deep heart is terrifying. We feel exposed and vulnerable and become paralyzed with fear. We run into hiding, covering ourselves with powerful defense mechanisms in order to keep safe: safe and protected from the pain of rejection, hoping that no one finds out and exposes the truth of who we really are. The shame would be unbearable if they knew that … **I'm not perfect**, and therefore, **I'm unworthy to receive your love!**

The truth of the matter is, we are worthy because God says we are. He never changed the way He looked at us; we did. We are still a reflection of His perfect image, warts and all. He meant it when He created us and said, 'It was good.' God's mirror produced a perfect image, His image of us. Our mirror on the other hand is cracked. We see imperfection and brokenness and mostly warts. We see it in ourselves, and we see it in each other.

One of the ways we learn who we are is through the mirroring of others. Our parents and families have the greatest influence over our lives, reflecting daily the truth (as they see it) about who we are. Every family has its cracks. There isn't one family on planet earth that has a perfect mirror. It doesn't matter what family you were born into, or adopted into, we all have some level of brokenness and shame to deal with. There are also other important folks who have a tremendous influence in our lives. Teachers and friends, associates and pastors, can powerfully influence the views we have of ourselves. There are many people who enter our lives and create a lasting and life-long impression of who we think we are. We can either thank and bless them for this, or forgive them.

The truth about who we really are is ultimately God's truth. Our identity and inheritance, no matter what we were told or believe about ourselves, comes from Him. The Psalms are filled with promises of God's unconditional love and respect for us. Even if our father and mother forsake us, even if our dearest friend turns his heel against us, even if we are abandoned by a husband in our youth, God's love still stands. The Lord did say to us that,

'You shall know the truth and the truth shall set you free.'
(John 8:32)

The challenge of this statement is, that we must find out what His truth is about us **before** we can be set free. The identity and the inheritance He gave us, versus the identity and inheritance we receive from this world, is very different.

One of the most influential places where we learn about God's truth is in the church. Unfortunately, most church families aren't very different from our families of origin. We still have the same shame-based fractured view of ourselves, each other and God when we gather together each week. Why would we feel or think or behave any differently just because we entered the door of a church building? We're the same people, with the same beliefs no matter where we are. We may act differently depending on where we are, but that's called pretending. The reason the church is so powerful, and the position of the pastor so influential, is because we sit and listen each week to messages that can transform our lives. And we in turn, can affect and transform our communities. We are converted and influenced to think differently about ourselves, each other and God. Hopefully the church family you've chosen is mirroring, as accurately as it possibly can, a true reflection of the image of God.

The Bible tells us to examine everything carefully and hold on to only that which is intrinsically, right and true (1 Thessalonians 5:21). It is important, even in our church family, to examine what we learn and what we've been taught. Just like our own well-meaning parents, our pastors and leaders also see life through the reflection of a broken mirror. It is absolutely critical for the health and well-being of your soul, to ask and seek and find God's truth about who He is, who you are and how you are to live. The Lord said that if we hold onto His teachings, we will know the truth and His truth will set us free. In our churches, we have given the pastor a position of authority and power to influence our beliefs and actions in many ways. No one, except our families, has this kind of jurisdiction over our lives. For those pastors who have mirrored health and healing and love into our lives, we will for eternity be grateful.

The pastors who abused their position of power and

authority in order to control and manipulate the sheep, are called Pharisees. They are blind guides, hypocritical and unclean. Jesus warned us to be careful, to be on guard against the yeast of the Pharisees and Sadducees. Their religious beliefs are so lethal, so cracked and distorted, they literally shut out the kingdom of heaven in men's faces. When shepherds exploit and control their congregations through shame-based religious teaching, it is as harmful as physical, verbal or emotional abuse. Just as physical abuse often results in bruised bodies, spiritual and pastoral abuse leaves scars on the psyche and soul. It is inflicted by persons who are accorded respect and honor in our society by virtue of their role as religious leaders and models of spiritual authority. They base that authority on the Bible, the Word of God, and see themselves as shepherds with a sacred trust. But when they violate that trust, when they abuse their authority and when they misuse ecclesiastical power to control and manipulate the flock, the results can be catastrophic.[5]

We've learned that almost all shame-bound families have similar characteristics and beliefs. We know this through years of studying alcoholics and their families. Similarly, families that are relatively shame-free and well-functioning share similar characteristics and beliefs. It is important to examine these patterns because the 'apple doesn't fall far from the tree'. We can easily be attracted to, or reproduce the same fruit we are familiar with. Whether it was in our church or our family, the roots of our twisted shame-based messages produce lethal fruit that affects our thinking, our loyalty to others, and the legacies we pass on to the next generation.

Lethal Logic

The very first place to look for a rotten root is the place where we hold all our beliefs and perceptions – they are all contained in our minds. Our thoughts and our truths make up the very core of how we view ourselves and the world in which we live. The more shame we inherited, the more lethal our thinking becomes. Proverbs teaches us that however a man thinks, so he is. It's true. In fact, scientists have proved what the Lord has known about us all along. Our thoughts actually control our feelings and behavior. This is why it is so important that we know what the truth is about who we are and who He is. Beliefs trigger emotions, and emotions trigger behavior. In order to change how you feel, you must change your thinking first.

The Lord said in Romans 12:

> *'... in view of God's grace offer your bodies as living sacrifices, holy and pleasing to God, which is your spiritual worship. Do not conform any longer to the patterns of this world, but be transformed by the renewing of your mind.'*

By renewing our minds and conforming to His truth, we will know the truth and the truth will set us free. Lethal thinking produces lethal feelings which produce lethal behavior. Renewing your lethal shame-bound thinking is the most important gift you can give yourself.

Lethal Loyalty

If our thinking is stinking, it will permeate into every relationship we have. The shame-based messages we grew up with, whether in our church or family, produced lethal loyalties to the people around us. We learned that being loyal to the family and to the family rules, were more important that being loyal to the truth. All families have rules and beliefs which they live by. These beliefs or traditions are usually passed down from one generation to the next. They are caught, not taught. We watch and learn from our family what is safe and appropriate behavior. These traits are what make your family unique. It's the same in a church family. The church system has rules and beliefs that are unique and sacred to its members. We learn about these rules and beliefs through Sunday school, church services and

Bible studies. What we learn becomes what we pass on from one generation to the next.

Shame-bound families, at home or at church, operate from the same set of rules. These rules keep the family looking perfect and problem free. The first rule is: be blind. No matter what is going on around us, we must keep up the perfect family (church) image. Ignore whatever is going on around you. It will eventually go away. The second rule is: be quiet. Every family has skeletons in their closet somewhere. No matter what, no one is allowed to talk about it. Everyone sees the pink elephant in the room, but no one has the permission to say it's there. Keep the family secret a secret. Rule three: be numb. Because no one is allowed to see or say there's a problem, no one is allowed to feel anything about it either. If you feel anger or pain, find a way to numb out. Rule four: be careful. Be careful not to trust anyone or let them too close. They may find out how awful we really are. They may expose the truth. Rule five: be good.[6] Since a shame-based family must look and act perfectly, the best way to pull this off is to become a good boy or a good girl. If you're really good, you can become the hero in the family, and that's even better. Your 'perfection' will distract the rest of the family from their imperfection. In the same way, if you're really bad, the family can blame all their problems on you so they won't have to feel their shame.

Because we follow the shame-based family rules, we can become more loyal to the family and family secrets than we are to ourselves, and even God. We know the consequences for breaking the silence. Instead of standing up for the truth, we become lethally loyal to the system. We would rather keep the peace in the family than break the rules, as if our life somehow depends on it.

Lethal Legacies

Because we don't break away from lethal logic and lethal loyalty, we pass our sin down from one generation to the next. Patterns are formed and family history is permanently recorded. In my family, one trait I inherited was an overwhelming feeling of shame. It lingered around for as far back as I can remember. When I became a Christian in high school, the thought that kept going over and over in my mind was, 'If God loves me, I must be OK.' The Lord is in the business of setting captives free from a heritage that is not His. He was healing my lethal family legacy of shame. He was renewing my lethal thinking. I didn't learn this because of a sermon I heard or a tape I listened to. It was because the God of the universe loved me enough to set me free.

It is important to listen to the voice of the Shepherd. He calls His own sheep by name and leads them out. His sheep follow Him because they know His voice. We have all lived with family legacies and church traditions for so long, we are hard of hearing and cannot discern His voice of truth from the legacies of lies we believe.

Lethal License

When your shame is blinding, and you think you are perfect and problem free, you probably believe you have the license to abuse and control whoever you want. Jesus described these leaders as Pharisees, blind guides and hypocrites. These abusive leaders believed they were above the law and had a legal license from God Almighty to judge, harm and shame anyone who tampered with their authority and power. Pastor Ken Blue describes the symptoms of spiritual abusive leaders which combines all three lethal components (logic, loyalty and legacies) from Matthew 23:

1) Abusive leaders base their spiritual authority on their positions or office rather than on their service to the group. Their style of leadership is authoritarian.
2) Leaders in shame-based churches often say one thing but do another. Their words and deeds do not match.
3) They manipulate people by making them feel guilty for not measuring up spiritually. They lay heavy religious

loads on people and make no effort to lift those loads. You know that you are in an abusive church if the loads just keep getting heavier.

4) Abusive leaders are preoccupied with looking good. They labor to keep up appearance. They stifle any criticism that puts them in a bad light.

5) They seek horrific titles and special privileges that elevate them above the group. They promote a class system with themselves at the top.

6) Their communication is not straight. Their speech becomes especially vague and confusing when they are defending themselves.

7) They major on minor issues to the neglect of the truly important one. They are conscientious about religious details but neglect God's larger agendas.[7]

Lethal Love

Shame-based churches produce shame-based people who cannot know or experience the true love of God. Shame poisons our ability to have a grace-filled love relationship with the Lord. Shame is the antithesis of the reflection of the *Imago Dei*. It produces the exact opposite mirrored image of God's character. This is lethal love. It is toxic, and poisons our ability to have a grace-filled love relationship with the Lord and with each other. It keeps us bound and dedicated to obeying religious rules in order to earn our love from the Father. It's no wonder that Jesus was angry with the Pharisees. They were actively and knowingly making people sick, when He came to heal the broken-hearted and set the captives free.

Notes

1. Robert Fulghn, *All I Really Need To Know I Learned In Kindergarten*.
2. Sandra Wilson, Ph.D., *Released from Shame*, Downers Grove, Illinois: InterVarsity Press, 1990, p. 25.

3. Gershin Kaufman, cited in John Bradshaw, *Bradshaw on the Family*, Deerfield Beach, Florida: Health communications 2.

4 Don Williams, *Jesus and Addiction: A Prescription to Transform the Dysfunctional Church and Recover Authentic Christianity*, San Diego, California: Recovery Publications, 1993, p. 35.

5. Ron Enroth, *Churches That Abuse*, Grand Rapids: Zondervan, 1992, p. 2.

6. Sandra Wilson, Ph.D., *Shame Free Parenting*, Downers Grove, Illinois: InterVarsity Press, 1992, pp. 19–21.

7. Ken Blue, *Healing Spiritual Abuse, How to Break Free from Bad Church Experiences*, Downers Grove, Illinois: InterVarsity Press, 1993, pp. 134–135.

Chapter 12

The Freedom of Forgiveness

'To err is human, to forgive divine.'
(Alexander Pope, *Essay on Criticism*)

' "I can forgive, but I cannot forget" is only another way of saying "I cannot forgive!" ' (Henry Ward Beecher)

'Then Peter came to Jesus and asked, "Lord, how many times shall I forgive my brother when he sins against me? Up to seven times?" Jesus answered, "I tell you, not seven times, but seventy-seven times." ' (Matthew 18:21–22)

'Father, forgive them, for they do not know what they are doing.' (Jesus Christ, while being crucified)

The purpose of this chapter is two-fold; first, to help those who are currently in an abusive religious system put things into proper perspective. Secondly, for those who have previously been in an abusive situation, as well as those who currently are in one, to successfully walk out of the chains of abuse. The previous eleven chapters may have been of help to the reader so far, but without really applying this chapter the help will either be minimal or fade away entirely.

There are laws, or principles, in the universe which are non-negotiable. Gravity would be such a law. Anyone, no matter where they are at in the universe, is affected second by second by the ongoing effects of gravity. We now know of and understand the reality of gravity. Some four hundred years ago no one had heard of gravity. Despite not understanding the principle of it, the laws of gravity were still very much in effect. 2000 years ago people knew that if they stepped off a cliff the landing could be rather serious depending on the height of the cliff. Gravity is less noticeable, but just as real, in different parts of the universe. Astronauts who have visited the moon have noticed, for example, that the immediate effects of gravity are much less. They are able to jump higher and longer than on earth, When landing the effects are less as well, although to leap of a high cliff would be dangerous on the moon as well as on the earth. It is just less noticeable on the moon.

In a similar way God's law of forgiveness is vitally important for all human beings. It is usually not until one becomes a follower of Christ, however, that the true effects of forgiveness, anger, and judgement are realized. The principles are still the same but the laws of forgiveness are much more noticeable in the spirit realm than in the natural. Even in the natural realm, however, doctors and psychologists have noticed the long-term benefits of living with attitudes of forgiveness as opposed to being filled with bitterness and anger. A local doctor, Grant Mullen, Md. who has a mental health practice in Hamilton, Ontario, states that:

> 'People who continue to live with unresolved emotional issues are very much prone to stress induced medical symptoms. Oftentimes the effects of long term emotional issues, such as anger or bitterness, can result in chronic pain, sickness, and fatigue.'

For the Christian, though, God's laws of forgiveness become more black and white and much more immediate. The point being that once an individual chooses to come under the salvation and lordship of Jesus Christ, forgiveness becomes much less of an option, although it never really was optional, merely less noticeable. Forgiveness becomes a critical principle of life that, like gravity, can only be set aside by those who ignore the very real consequences of withholding it.

Forgiveness is one of the primary themes of the Bible. Forgiveness by a loving God who so loved the world that He gave His only begotten Son to die on a cross for payment of our sins. Often ignorant critics of Christianity think of the Bible as being hopelessly unrealistic and out of touch with humanity and where society is really at. The opposite is actually the case. The Bible is filled with story after story of men and women who loved God, but who fell very short of living lives of perfect holiness. In fact, God seems to almost delight in pointing out some of the flaws and sins of some of the greatest heroes of the Bible such as David and Gideon. The point being made, over and over again, is that God is a God who is a *'compassionate and gracious God, slow to anger, abounding in love and faithfulness, maintaining love to thousands, and forgiving wickedness, rebellion and sin'* (Exodus 34:6–7). We, as fallen humanity, are incapable of living in complete holiness. We are in deep need of the grace of God.

God loves it when we make choices in life based on desiring to please Him. None the less, He also makes it startlingly clear that the only hope man can have of an ongoing relationship with Him is because of His loving and forgiving nature. Here lies part of the great danger for those who have been hurt by other Christians, especially for a prolonged period of time by church leaders.

The State of Grace

Another ongoing principle in both the natural and the supernatural realms is the law of reciprocity. In fact, one of the first laws students of physics learn is that **for every action there is an equal and opposite reaction.** The parallel principle in the Kingdom of God is simply that you cannot keep what you do not give away. Essentially this has to do with the very nature of God. Since the essence of God is love, He constantly gives away His best, such as Jesus, for those who are completely unworthy. So, when Jesus taught the disciples the principles of prayer He stated that if *'you do not forgive men their sins, your Father will not forgive your sins'* (Matthew 6:15). Likewise, it is impossible to say we only love God. The first commandment to love the Lord our God with everything is inseparable from the second, which is to love our neighbor as ourselves. It is impossible for us to live alone in a grace-based relationship with God. Just as we receive grace and mercy from God so we must also extend it. The apostle John put it this way:

> *'If anyone says, "I love God," yet hates his brother, he is a liar. For anyone who does not love his brother, whom he has seen, cannot love God, whom he has not seen. And he has given us this command: Whoever loves God must also love his brother.'*   (1 John 4:20–21)

The problem faced by many is that they want to be recipients of grace and mercy but they refuse to dispense grace and mercy. Jesus gave clear warning of the dangers of trying to do so, in the parable of the king and his slaves in Matthew 18, verses 23–35. The king demanded that one of his slaves who owed him money be thrown into debtors prison until he could pay off the debt. The slave cried out and appealed to the king's mercy. The king *'felt compassion and released him and forgave him the debt'* (verse 27). Note that the king not only released him from the prison sentence but forgave him the debt as well. The amount owed, ten thousand talents, was equivalent to millions and millions of dollars in today's money. This is a picture of our sins against God. Even the most righteous of us is guilty and completely unworthy of God and His love. Yet because of Jesus' work of atonement our sins are separated from us far as the east is from the west.

The slave however did not extend that grace and compassion towards those that were in debt to himself. He found one of his fellow slaves who owed him a hundred denarii, approximately one hundred days worth of wages. He demanded that his co-worker pay the amount and even began to choke him. The fellow slave asked for patience in order to pay him back. He refused to extend mercy and had him thrown in jail. In God's eyes this is how we appear when we ask for His forgiveness but refuse to extend it to others who have sinned against us.

Often, we give two basic justifications for not wanting to forgive. Many a time we exclaim 'But, you don't really understand what they did to me.' That can be true. It can be very difficult to put ourselves in the shoes of someone else and really appreciate the depths of their pain and suffering. Secondly, when we are wronged we frequently feel we have the right to withhold mercy due to our innocence, whether real or imagined. There is, however, one who not only can fully relate to our pain and rejection but who innocently suffered in a way beyond what we can ever completely comprehend.

When Jesus was dying on the cross of asphyxiation, gasping for breath, struggling to raise His body on nails driven through His feet, His cry was not from the pain, but due to His separation at that moment from the Father. Paul wrote:

> *'God made Him who had no sin to be sin for us, so that in Him we might become the righteousness of God.'*
>
> (2 Corinthians 5:21)

For a period of time the wrath of God towards sin came upon His precious and holy Son. The anguish of that separation, albeit brief, is unimaginable. Jesus, being the only begotten Son of God, was from the beginning with God and was God. The heartcry of Jesus throughout His days on the earth was constantly to please the Father by doing the things He saw the Father doing. He never initiated things on His own. He was never interested in doing His own thing. His food was pleasing the Father, even at the cost of His own dignity and life. It is not possible for us to really understand the pain He and the Father suffered at that moment. Never before, and probably never again, will the universe hear such a heart-rending cry of pain as when Jesus cried out, *'My God, my God, why have you forsaken me?'* Many humans have suffered terrible pain and suffering. None, however, have ever suffered so innocently, purely as a willing act of sacrifice for the cause of love.

As Jesus continued the parable He said that when the king found out that the slave had thrown the fellow slave in jail he, the king, then *'handed him over to the torturers until he should repay all that was owed him.'* I do not believe this parable is saying a Christian can lose their salvation. But I do believe it clearly indicates that a Christian who demands justice will end up receiving justice. Jesus stated in at least two different teaching times, that if we do not forgive those who have sinned against us neither can the Father forgive us our sins. In fact, this parable categorically demonstrates that we can nullify to a degree the full benefits of the cross when we demand justice.

The Kingdom of God, as Paul stated, is a realm of *'right-eousness, peace, and joy'* (Romans 14:17). When we do not reciprocate God's grace and mercy to others we, at least to some degree, prevent God from blessing us to the extent He desires. Jesus stated that He came that we might have life and have it abundantly. Many Christians, however, seem to experience only slight amounts of God's peace and joy. I believe one of the chief reasons for the discrepancy between the promise and our actual experience is our refusal to extend forgiveness.

I have used the phrase several times so far that 'hurting people end up hurting others if they do not get healed.' History shows that children abused by a father, who do not choose to forgive him, end up doing similar things to their own children. When we hear of a man who physically or sexually abused his children and was himself abused as a child, we are aghast! How could he behave that way, when he, himself, went through the pain, trauma, and shame? The reason is that we usually become what we rebel against.

The first commandment with a promise is to honor our mother and father that it would go well with us all the days of our life. When we choose not to forgive, the anger and bitterness inside of us goes so deep it becomes a 'bitter root'. The writer of Hebrews said:

> *'See to it that no one misses the grace of God and that no bitter root grows up to cause trouble and defile many.'*
> (Hebrews 12:15)

When the heart and soul become filled with anger and bitterness it is comparable to a physical body suffering from a growing cancer. It effects the whole of the organism. Proverbs 4, verse 23 reads:

> *'Above all else, guard your heart, for it is the wellspring of life.'*

Jesus stated that:

> *'The good man brings good things out of the good stored up in his heart, and the evil man brings evil things out of the evil stored up in his heart. For out of the overflow of his heart his mouth speaks.'*

When we are walking in our King's righteousness (God's will) His Kingdom is realized in part by experiencing His divine peace and joy in the Holy Spirit. When we choose not to forgive others, as in the parable, we can be handed over to the torturers. The torturers for us can be anything from lack of God's peace to possibly tormenting spirits. I am not saying a Christian can be demon-possessed. That would be a contradiction in terms. But in areas where a Christian is practising lawlessness, as with maintaining anger and bitterness, we can open ourselves up to demonic affliction.

We do need to realize two things regarding sins of the heart. First anger, bitterness and other sins of the heart are very real and serious sins towards God and man. Jesus stated that to even look on a woman with lust, was as if we had already sexually sinned. Jesus stated that merely to be angry towards a brother in one's heart was subject to judgment. Whoever says to someone ' *"You fool!" will be in danger of the fire of hell'* (Matthew 5:22). Secondly, sin is Satan's legal domain. When a Christian chooses not to walk in the Kingdom of God we are by choice choosing to walk in Satan's domain. Our sins, in general may be forgiven, but we are called to daily make choices honoring to God. Many Christians forfeit their right to the fullness of the peace and joy the Holy Comforter longs to give us. Instead we can actually be making room for a tormenting, or 'torturing' spirit to afflict us until we are ready to submit to God's word and will for our lives. We can belong to God but still not attempt to surrender every area of our lives to Him. We can belong to God, but we can have 'rooms' in the 'house of our heart' that are not clean and swept out.

The writer of Hebrews stated that in Christ Jesus we have a high priest who can relate to our temptations, including anger and bitterness (Hebrews 2:17–18). In our situations of being wronged, at best we are sometimes more a victim than perpetrator. But very rarely, where human conflict is involved, are we ever completely innocent. But in Christ coming and dying for our sins He was more than innocent – He was completely righteous in all of His being. In light of the forgiveness the true King, God has extended to Christians through Jesus' work of atonement, we no longer have the right to hang on to anger or bitterness towards others.

'Blessed are the peacemakers for they shall be called the sons of God'

In the parable, despite the fact that the king forgave the first slave his huge debt, the slave then proceeded to choke the one who owed him a comparatively minor amount. One of the chief characteristics of truly born again Christians, should not only be peace, but a pattern of building and healing relationships: relationship between different ethnic groups, between different generations, and especially between man and God. We are called 'Christians' – followers, or disciples of Christ (Acts 11:26). For those who take on the name of the Lord Jesus, a chief characteristic of our lives should be His characteristic of not only forgiving but bridging the gap between God and man. One of the reasons Jesus was such a threat to the religious leaders of His time was that He crossed over the barriers and went to the outcasts, such as the prostitutes and thieves. Peace is not just an aspect of Jesus – it is deep within the core of His being. We read in Luke chapter 23, verse 34 of Jesus while in intense pain on the cross praying, *'Father, forgive them, they know not what they do!'* If those who consider themselves to be followers of Jesus cannot choose to forgive those who have sinned against them, then we are not true disciples of the Lord Jesus.

In fact, not only does God call us to forgive those who sin against us, but He calls us to **bless them**! Jesus said:

'You have heard that it was said, "Love your neighbor and hate your enemy." But I tell you: Love your enemies and pray for those who persecute you, that you may be sons of your Father in heaven.' (Matthew 5:43–45)

It is so very hard for us to fathom the depths of God's heart because we are in the process of unlearning the ways of this world system. But, the heart, or essence, of God is love. A powerful love that forgives and does not take into account a wrong suffered. So often, even as Christians, we say we forgive but we want to keep a secret tab of how many times so and so has sinned against us. That only goes to show that we have not really forgiven, if we have not chosen to let it go. When Peter asked the Lord Jesus, *' "Lord, how many times shall I forgive my brother when he sins against me?" Up to seven times?" Jesus answered, "I tell you, not seven times, but seventy-seven times"'* (Matthew 18:21–22). The number was so ridiculously high that obviously no one could keep track.

One of names the Bible gives Satan is 'the accuser'. Satan is the one who is constantly trying to accuse us of our sins before God. What many Christians do not realize is that Satan is very much a legalist. He knows far more than we do of God's laws. He loves to not only tempt Christians into sin, but to then manipulate them into feelings of futility with the guilt, sin, shame, and condemnation. When we hang onto other's sins we are, in deed, serving the accuser, more than we are the Lord Jesus Christ.

As with the unmerciful servant, we too can end up 'choking' our brothers and sisters in Christ. One of the most important functions we can perform in representing Christ is to simply minister forgiveness. Not only one to another for sins against each other, but in the overall ministry of reconciliation between God and man. Shortly after His resurrection, Jesus breathed the Holy Spirit on the disciples and told them, *'If you forgive anyone his sins, they are forgiven; if you do not forgive them, they are not forgiven.'* When we legalistically stand on our imagined right to demand justice, not only do we rob ourselves of God's complete blessings but in effect we can be spiritually 'choking' our brother. We can end up robbing them by actually playing the part of an accuser rather than representing the nature of our Lord Jesus.

'Do not judge lest ... '

A final thought on the wrong of holding others in judgment, is that we can actually be presuming on the role of Jesus Himself. In John 5:22–23 we read these words of Jesus:

> *' ... the Father judges no one, but has entrusted all judgment to the Son, that all may honor the Son just as they honor the Father. He who does not honor the Son does not honor the Father, who sent him.'*

The Father, in His love for the Son has given Him the sole honor of judge of all. When we insist on judging those who have sinned against us we ourselves are guilty ourselves of sinning against our Lord Jesus. This, of course, does not include properly appointed judges of the land who are part of a nation's legal system. Those judges, in fact, whether they realize it or not, are part of God's authority in bringing about righteousness (1 Peter 2:13–14). Neither does it include church leaders who at times must discern the heart and motivation of some before releasing them into authority or ministry, or on occasion into church discipline. Whom it does concern is all of us in choosing either to choke people with guilt or bless them with forgiveness. And herein is the spiritual application of the law of reciprocity. If we extend mercy we shall be shown mercy (Matthew 5:7). If, however, we judge and choose not to forgive, we shall be judged (Matthew 7:1).

> 'This is how my heavenly Father will treat each of you unless you forgive your brother from your heart.'
> (Matthew 18:35)

Seasons of Forgiveness

Having stated the importance of forgiving those who may have spiritually abused us, it is also important to state that walking out of the hurt and anger of spiritual abuse will probably not be a quick decision nor a one-time act. To be completely set free from the trauma of being hurt by spiritual leaders whom we have trusted, will definitely be a process, as opposed to a simple event. The more serious and long-term the abuse, the more long-term the season. One good friend of mine who went through incredible church abuse found that for several years afterwards, she would sometimes begin to shake from fear when she walked into a church building – even if she knew that church to be healthy.

It is essential to understand that we are not pure spirit, neither are we pure intellect. We are body, soul, and spirit. The soul includes not only the intellect and the memories, but the emotions as well. Many want to downplay the importance of emotions. Emotions are a gift from God that help make life worth living. Our emotions allow us to enjoy life, one another, and God. It is through the emotions that we can be stirred to raise ourselves out of apathy and into action. It is through the emotions that we can experience pain, which is also a gift from God. Without the emotions, we would be little more that robots programmed to perform.

The emotions, likewise, should not be confused with the spirit. One can be going through pain, sorrow, or a grieving process but still experience God's peace which passes all comprehension (Philippians 4:7). We can daily experience God's strength in our lives via the joy of the Holy Spirit (Nehemiah 8:10), but still grieve over loss or hurt from pain. A Christian who has just lost a mate or child can go through a real season of grieving for the loss but also rejoice over knowing that they are now with Jesus. As the author of Ecclesiastes put it:

> *'There is a time for everything, and a season for every activity under heaven: a time to be born and a time to die, a time to plant and a time to uproot, a time to kill and a time to heal, a time to tear down and a time to build, a time to weep and a time to laugh, a time to mourn and a time to dance.'*
> (Ecclesiastes 3:1–4)

Our emotions are a wonderful gift and tool, but we are not to be dominated by them. Yet it is also a mistake to ignore or discount them. Like the comfort or warmth from being close to a flame, or the pain from being too close to a flame, our emotions can serve as an indicator of both blessings or danger. To attempt to negate the emotions is to cut ourselves off from a precious gift from God.

One of the most hurtful emotions we can experience is rejection. Because God is so faithful in His love we probably were not made to undergo serious rejection such as divorce from a mate, or abuse or abandonment by parents. Serious spiritual abuse by a church leader we have respected, followed, and perhaps loved is not unlike the abuse of children by a trusted parent or adult. It is not only abuse but a betrayal of a special trust. It would be a serious mistake to underestimate the damage and disillusionment that can come to a soul through a long process of violated trust and abuse. At the same time, it would be a serious mistake for the victim to remain a victim by choosing to either not forgive the abuser and/or not to reach out to God. It helps to realize that even though leaders may be God's delegated leaders they are, as we all are, at best imperfect representations of His goodness.

Therefore, when one begins to walk away from a spiritually abusive situation most likely forgiveness and complete freedom will be a process and not merely a one-time choice. Just as the hurt came over a period of time, so will the healing, although it may not take as long. The first step, however, is simply to make the choice that one will move on in God's grace. The devil's temptation will be to hang on to our anger, hurt, and disillusionment and say 'what's the point of trying again.' Almost everyone who has ever been shattered by a terrible divorce has faced that same lie. Many who have refused to believe that lie have gone on to enjoy wonderful new relationships.

Many think that we need a mountain of faith to move a mere mustard seed. But God knows our frailties and merely requires a mustard seed of faith to move a mountain. In the initial period of grief, anger, and confusion following abuse, it would be a mistake to expect a quick release of the anger or hurt. The key, however, is to take what faith we have in God and His word, and make choices to surrender to Him. Even in the midst of overwhelming pain one can purely by faith begin to ask God for the necessary grace to forgive. Or even to ask Him for faith to continue on and move towards His will is a step of obedience. God is so faithful that even when we are unable to really forgive or to walk in faith, if we will humble ourselves and confess our need for grace, strength, and an obedient heart, He will begin to release us into the process of healing. Even when we think we have no faith, we can utilize that mustard seed by merely asking God for faith and grace. It is important to remember that even the longest journeys always start with a very simple first step.

How long will the healing take? Those who were raised in healthy families and have a strong sense of security and significance will bounce back quicker than others. Those that came into the abusive system with hurts, wounds, and bad self-images to begin with, will probably take longer to heal. The more time spent in giving your heart and soul to a system, the more time the healing of anger and an over-whelming sense of loss will take.

One of the keys is to realize the nature of toxic faith systems. They are usually made up of individuals who derive their self-worth out of their performance. When that is the case it important to let God heal us of our 'religious habits' as well as some of our faulty theology. For example, if the leaders constantly impressed you that you were in sin if you did not attend every church meeting and function, then you need to learn that God is a 24-hour a day God. He is not the God of meetings and programs but the God of life. For many in highly structured abusive systems a good idea might be to start being creative on Sunday mornings. Instead of immediately trying to go to a new church on Sunday morning try going instead to the beach or a quiet place with your Bible, and meditate on the Psalms or one of the Gospels. This could be very helpful if the idea of Sunday morning church fills you with overwhelming fear or depression. Try having a late breakfast with your whole family and spend some time reading a passage of scripture and praying together. If you have been abused by a church, likely as not your children have also suffered as well. They, as well as you, might need to learn that Jesus really did come so that you might have abundant life. Learn as a family that having fun together and enjoying your love, is as important to God as the more 'serious' things. If your prayer time has evolved into a time of striving to get God to do things, try to just spend time thanking Him for the simple things that you **are** grateful for, such as your health, or finances, or the friends that really care about you. Thank Him for Jesus, the cross, and your eternal inheritance. For those readers who find themselves in this place I would thoroughly recommend Lauren Sandford's book *The Wounded Warrior*. The author helps us to realize we often inadvertently put relating to God into religious formulas.

I am not saying anyone abused should never attend church again. Neither am I saying that we should never again become involved in serious intercession or good works. But often in the initial stage of the healing process we need to get back to the basics of allowing ourselves to be loved by God and relearning our first love for Him – devoid of all the programs. Some would say at this point, that if one is empty one should immediately start serving, so that it will come back pressed down and in good measure. The problem is, however, that you cannot give away what you do not have! Before Jesus said to His disciples, *'freely, freely you have received, freely, freely give,'* they had spent several seasons merely walking with Him and freely (with no strings attached) receiving from Him.

A second stage will possibly be learning to trust Christians again. Isolation is a powerful tool Satan uses to keep his discouraging lies from being exposed to God's light. If you still have friends from your church, or in the local Christian community, that you are on good terms with, seek them out and spend time with them. You don't have to do anything religious. Rather just be with them and allow in a very natural way for the love and light of God in them to strengthen and refresh you. Go out to dinner or watch a movie together. Learn again to rejoice in God's gift of friendship without any necessary 'ministry' agenda attached to it.

More likely than not there is a large church in your community where you can go for a while anonymously. I am not saying one should never re-enter true church fellowship. But there is a re-entry process into the Christian community. After focusing on a few good Christian friend-ships, find a church where you can simply go and worship the Lord. After all, this is what we were made for. Even more than our Martha-service, God wants our hearts, like Mary (Luke 10:38–42). Let the preaching minister to you and where it is not perhaps quite applicable to your situation don't worry about it. Trust God that the good work He has begun in you, He will complete (Philippians 1:6), even if you can't see how at that particular moment.

As you learn to trust God and other Christians again, seek a 'safe place' where you can share your heart. Your friends may or may not be able to give you healing counseling, but just being able to have someone listen to you without judging or condemning will be helpful. As it says in Proverbs 27:6:

> *'Faithful are the wounds of a friend.'* (NAS)

Sometimes the simple prayer offered up in love and faith can be far more effective than the sophisticated prayers of an 'expert or professional'. If you can locate a counseling ministry in your community or a local church that is experienced in the area of spiritual abuse, they could be of great benefit in helping to put things into perspective and guiding you through the healing process.

Essentially though, there are two important understand-ings to keep in mind. More likely than not, your healing will be a process. **Don't** pressure yourself by falling into the same old patterns of religious behavior and think that God dislikes you if you are not serving, serving, serving! A great athlete who has severely damaged his knee first needs surgery and then the process of therapy before he can come back up to standard. The same is true of your situation, perhaps even more so since your heart has been wounded. Secondly, and equally important, **don't** let yourself live the rest of your life as a perpetual victim. Every promise in the Bible is still very true. God knew before the foundations of the world that the bride of Christ would have all sorts of growing pains and make mistakes while growing up. But His promises for you are still very much alive and true. Jesus did come for you that you might have life and have it abundantly. You are the apple of your heavenly Father's eye and He longs to give you more of His Kingdom.

As you begin to start asking God to forgive those who have hurt you, Satan will most likely attempt to use the following strategy. On Monday you might spend time earnestly praying into the past situation. You will have confessed to God your anger towards certain individuals and leaders. Most likely, you will sense at least some relief from that pain and hurt as God takes the burden and replaces it with His peace, joy, and righteousness. A couple of days will pass and then maybe at work you will have a stressful day. At the height of the stress the temptation to get angry and blow up will come. But, it will probably be tied into your 'old' anger towards the former leaders. The lie will be 'my life is hopelessly in shambles and it's all their fault! There's no way I can ever forgive them.' Remember that besides Satan being the accuser he is also a liar. In fact, Jesus said that *'he* (Satan) *is the father of lies'* (John 8:44). Lying is one of his chief tactics in blocking us from going deeper into the freedom of the gospel. So expect Satan to attempt to destroy your confidence in the ongoing healing God gives you.

Often in going through a season of healing the Lord will deal with us as if we were an onion. He will peal off one layer at a time and each layer can cause us to cry. So it can be true that it might take several, if not many, sessions of prayer, forgiveness, and repentance before we are finally free. But don't buy the lie of the enemy that nothing was accomplished or gained by the recent times of confession. A trick of mine, when the enemy brings on thoughts of anger towards someone I know I have forgiven, is at that precise moment to pray prayers of blessing upon the person. Pray for their heart, their families, their finances, and their ministry. Pray that God would cause their souls to prosper.

When we do that in the face of temptation to be angry, Satan's plan backfires on him.

When you pray for that pastor, or brother, or sister who has hurt you, pray prayers for them as you would want them to pray for you if the situation was reversed. Don't pray prayers of witchcraft such as 'God judge them and don't let them off the hook.' Remember that's the role of Satan, the accuser.

A final suggestion concerning the journey towards complete forgiveness would be to not let the dark memories completely cover up all of the goodness in where you have been. Very few abusive church situations are completely black and white. Most of us would not really have been drawn into the toxic system we were in if there were not some very positive aspects about the church or ministry. I remember with fondness a pastor I was under for a few years, long ago. I finally was no longer able to take any sort of leadership role in the church because of problems stemming from his immaturity in a few basic areas. To some degree I myself had been hurt. But at the same time, that period of learning and ministry in my life was overall a very positive time. In fact, that pastor was continually an encouragement to me to really go for God with all my heart, and not to compromise. I am grateful for the lessons and encouragement that pastor gave to me.

When we take the long view of an abusive leader, or parent, we can understand that in most cases they did the hurtful things they did not because they wanted to, but because they themselves are also victims. When we begin to see their hearts as God sees them, we can then begin to see past the temporalness of the pain. We can then authentically pray prayers for them with the motivation of God – love. And when we can begin to do that not only do we begin to reap what we sow, but more importantly we begin to reflect our heavenly Father.

God in His wisdom, love and grace has chosen not only to extend His being towards humanity, but also, to a degree, to express His love through humanity. Therein, lies not only opportunity for incredible joy, but also the possibility of extreme pain. It is only in a true, that is, a growing, surrender to His heart, truth and ways, that we can learn to be effectively not only givers of His love and grace, but recipients as well. For those who have liberally given their time, their money, and their talents to His people, seemingly only to receive pain, shame and frustration in return, perhaps these eternal words of Jesus are more necessary that ever:

> *'Blessed are the poor in spirit, for theirs is the kingdom of heaven. Blessed are those who mourn, for they shall be comforted. Blessed are the gentle, for they shall inherit the earth. Blessed are those who hunger and thirst for righteousness, for they shall be satisfied. Blessed are the merciful, for they shall receive mercy. Blessed are the pure in heart, for they shall see God. Blessed are the peacemakers, for they shall be called sons of God.'*   (Matthew 5:3–9)

Marc has served in various forms of church leadership for over 15 years, including teaching, preaching, counseling, evangelism, and church planting. For the last 14 years, Marc has mainly been working with Mantle of Praise Ministries on an international level, functioning in a prophetic 'Barnabus ministry' of encouragement. He has ministered in conferences, seminars, and churches in Scandinavia, Europe, Africa, Britain, North America, and Asia, traveling an average of four to five months a year. He is used by the Lord in a variety of denominations from Lutheran to Baptist, Pentecostal to Anglican. His underlying focus is basically in five areas: The Father-Heart of God, The Priesthood of the Believer, Unity in the Body of Christ, Restoration for the Traditional Churches, and Revival. Marc, his wife Kim, and their two daughters and one son reside in Toronto, Canada. Marc has functioned as an associate pastor with the Toronto Airport Christian Fellowship since 1992, when he has not been on the road. He is also the author of *The Elijah Years – Insights for the '90s*.